Caring Enough to Help the One You Love

Caring Enough to Help the One You Love

by
Richard Dortch

New Leaf Press

Other books by
Richard W. Dortch
Integrity, How I Lost It and My Journey Back
Fatal Conceit
Losing It All & Finding Yourself

First Edition
June 1994

Library of Congress Catalog Number: 93-87252
ISBN: 0-89221-259-4

Note: Some names have been changed to protect the identity
and privacy of those involved.

Dedication

This book is lovingly dedicated to those who helped me when my journey seemed so hard. To the thousands who prayed and wrote to me, to those who believed in me. Among them,

My father and mother
My brothers Ed, Charles, Kenneth, and their families
My sister, Mary Frances, and her family
Mildred's mother
Her sisters Rosalie and Delores, and their families
Her brothers Robert and Jerry, and their families
Dr. and Mrs. Charles Cookman
Dr. and Mrs. Gordon Matheny
My colleagues at Heritage Village Church:
Larry and Sandra Sims,
Shirley Fullbright,
Eric and Becky Watt, Leslie Jones, Gene Shelton,
Brad Bacon,
Mark Muirhead,
Brian and Esther Boone,
Vi and Eddie Azvedo,
Charlotte Whiting,
And a host of others who I love dearly.

Acknowledgments

I am a debtor to Tim Dudley, my publisher, of New Leaf Press. We have a friendship built on trust. In this, my fourth book for New Leaf Press, Tim shared my concern that we help hurting people who "care enough." The newest member of the team at New Leaf Press is Jim Fletcher. His help, hard work, and prayer for the project was outstanding. He would not let go of my vision for this book. Val Cindric, my editor, is a gift from God. She tends to bring my best out of my heart and mind. Becky, Judy, Joyce, and Jacqueline contributed greatly to this treatise. They are all professionals whom I esteem highly.

Contents

Preface

I am the most fortunate person to have someone love me. Her name is Mildred. I have never for a moment questioned or doubted her love for me. My life is fulfilled. Knowing God's love, and hers has been all that I could ask for. Our family went through five years of deep agony. Had not it been for God's grace and Mildred's love, our family could not have survived. I am sure it has been largely because of her that so many people have asked me, "How do you help someone you love?" They know, or have heard about her love and faithfulness to me. They saw how we survived. Now, many people come to us at our crisis agency seeking help. I often ask them why they come for help.

"We can trust you, Pastor — you had a failure. Your wife stood by your side. You admitted your mistake and God has restored you. We have all experienced that."

This book is very important to Mildred and me. We have searched our hearts, and now share with you how to face the great issues of life. I wanted you to know how you can clearly determine that the one you love is having a problem. We tell you how to detect the problem. Then how to walk with them through the difficult time. The most important thing we tell you is how to help them come out on the other side, the side of victory. There is help for all who seek.

How do you help someone you love? It is a piercing question. It is a question that I hear frequently. In counseling, in personal dialogue, and in ministry, I also hear the question on the late night call-in television program that I host for two hours each night in approximately 30 cities across America.

Through these simple truths may you find the peace, joy, and release that has come to us. If you are prepared to admit your need of help you'll find that much help and happiness awaits you through these pages. Always remember, you are loved.

Introduction

When the call came from Meredith, I knew she was deeply troubled.

"How can you help someone you love?" she asked. "I knew Joseph had some problems, but not 'those kinds.' I wish I had known what was happening. How could I have missed it? Why didn't I know something was wrong?"

That call, and many others like it, gave birth to this book. How can we know when the one we love is hurting? How can we know when someone we care about is failing, troubled, disillusioned, depressed, and giving up on life and themselves?

Every night, when I host a national television call-in program, I am confronted with people who need help — not only for themselves — but for someone they care about.

"Will you pray for me?" a boy named Ryan pleaded. "My father has been abusing me since my mother died. Pray that when he comes home tonight, he won't touch me. I love my dad, but I don't know what to do."

That is the question that demands an answer: I love my alcoholic father — or my elderly mother, my depressed wife, my cheating husband, my rebellious son, my wayward daughter — but I don't know what to do.

Since PTL and the events that changed my life, hundreds of hurting folks have come to us seeking a listening ear and an open heart for their own personal tragedies. In an effort to meet the ever-growing demand for help, we founded a crisis agency, Life Challenge. We walk with people through their crisis period. Everyone's problem is so different. No two problems are the same. We simply try to love them back to wholeness.

Humbled by the magnitude of the personal problems we encounter each day, our staff must seek the Father continually for the needs of broken, wounded souls. Life Challenge is an agency committed to caring for people in crisis.

Crisis. I know a lot about that.

When I was facing what could have been the destruction of my life, God loved me enough to hold me in His arms and comfort me. He loved me in spite of myself. I realized that my failures had resulted from the ugliness that first appeared when our common enemy fell from God's presence because he wanted to be equal with God.

Pride led me to several valleys and, although I had held positions of responsibility within my church, nothing could prevent my fall during the PTL scandal. I was shaken to my very soul.

Each member of my family, Mildred, our daughter Deanna, and our son Rich, stood by me with an unflinching resolve. Our daughter and son held us up emotionally at a time when our knees buckled under the weight of enormous troubles. They saw that their loved ones needed strength so badly. As we have been able to step out into the sunshine in recent years, we weep with joy and gratitude for the love our family provided for us.

God knows very well the tragedies that have ruptured the life of Richard Dortch. He knows my heart, my spirit, my intent. He knows my mind, and He knows my secrets.

People from all races and all walks of life are hurting because of unresolved problems and sin in their lives. The pain of personal crisis isn't partial to any one group; it exists in people, churches, businesses, schools, etc. I know because individuals all across our country come to Life Challenge seeking freedom from their burdens. We applaud those with the courage to come forward and seek solutions.

When our ministry staff gathers to study the individual cases that come to us at Life Challenge, we feel a tremendous burden in our spirit to help. Recently we asked, "How can we reach a wider area to let people know someone understands and wants to provide solutions?"

I believe I have been made to know that God wants me to write this book.

How do we help ourselves and the ones we love? Do we care enough to try? Should we get involved in their pain, or let them perish in their own hurts?

No, as Christians, we are called to the aid of the traveler who had been wounded on his journey through life — just as the Good Samaritan stopped to help the beaten man along the road. The tragedy may be the result of his own foolishness or caused by circumstances beyond his control. No matter. We must be willing to take the oil of healing and pour it into his wounds. Then, like the Good Samaritan, we must go one step further and meet his needs until he can stand on his own two feet.

Such a calling, however, takes courage, determination, and, most of all, love — the love that only Jesus can give.

Let us equip ourselves, know the signs, and have the sensitivity to know what is going on in the lives of those we love.

"If I would have only known how she felt," the distraught husband cried, "I would have spent more time with her. I didn't know."

"I couldn't tell," the sobbing wife stammers. "He means so much to me. Yet, I lost him because I did not know what was going on in his life. He's gone forever."

My prayer is that this book will equip you to recognize some of the signs that indicate trouble brewing in the lives of those you love. I also pray that you will have the wisdom and courage to confront yourself — and that loved one — with the truth.

If you are facing a burden so great that it feels as if everything is closing in around you, remember someone cares enough to help you.

Or, you may be on the other side of the barrier, and at a loss as to how to help someone you love — whether he or she is a family member or a friend. Just remember that our Father knows us by name and has the hairs on our heads numbered. The angels in heaven rejoice and wonder at the love God reserves for each individual on planet earth! He loves you and me.

In fact, He has provided compassion right here on earth for all of us. Compassion in the form of caring people who prayed for a wayward loved one. Compassion in the form of a brother or sister reaching out to a fallen person. It's that compassion that will help someone gripped with a problem in his or her life.

I care about you and the one you love. It is my sincere prayer that this book will in some way enable you to help someone you love.

Prayerfully read these pages, slowly, deliberately, with sensitivity. Read it for understanding, for encouragement, for instruction, for healing.

As you seek to help the one you love, I believe you will also receive help for yourself.

1

Growing Up . . . at Any Age

Perseverance must finish its work so that you may be mature and complete, not lacking anything.
James 1:4;NIV

As a teenager, I had known Ron for most of our lives. Although he was 26 and I was 16, he was my friend and I cared greatly about him. Articulate, smart, pleasant (when he wanted to be), Ron was a class act. I always admired him for his way with words.

Controversy, however, was his ally, and he loved a good fight. The smallest issue became for him a point of contention. He had to convince you that he was right about most things. He could walk into a calm, peaceful situation and in a short time have people at each others' throats.

He took sides on non-important issues, and you could easily offend him. As much as people loved him — and they did — he could not avoid confrontation. Some people became hostile and opposed him at every opportunity. Every experience for Ron was a cliffhanger.

After a long stint in his leadership position, he was fired from his very good job.

Years later our paths crossed, and he lamented to me the sorrows and hurts of his life. He had forsaken his wife, become involved with several women outside of his marriage, and now the world around him had crumbled. He was alone.

As we talked, I loved him enough to ask, "Why, why, why?"

"I never grew up, never assumed responsibility. Because I never learned to shut my mouth, I lost it all," Ron shared with me.

Sad, yes, but true.

Identifying Immaturity

When you picked up this book it was probably with the hope of helping someone you love with a problem. What do you expect to find at the root of his or her problem? Here are some possibilities. Chances are, the person you so desperately want to help has some difficulty with maturity. We must come to the realization that achieving maturity — on any level — is a journey we must all make. That is what life is about, understanding, growing up. As we make a real step to maturity, then release can come. We can be at peace with ourselves and others.

We see a continual stream of hurting folks who weep and grieve over situations that threaten to overtake their very existence. Many of these people have no idea where the root of their problem began. They just know the pain is now unbearable.

Can they look at themselves? Can they see if the problem originates within their own spirits? Seldom do they look inward, usually they are blaming others.

This is the critical truth we must identify. It is the key to understanding a personality problem.

A 47-year-old ad executive has three homes, a boat, fleets of cars, a picture-perfect family, and political connections, but he can't run forever from his infidelity problems.

Raised under his father's tutelage, learning the business and inheriting "the empire," he now finds it crumbling around him because of a lack of morality.

What caused the collapse? What caused the bleeding ulcer that finally hospitalized him?

Somewhere along the line, this man didn't grow up. He didn't mature.

On a sunny day, surrounded by smiling friends and enjoying his private tennis courts, this man clasped the hand of the devil, who told him that riches would suffice. He would never have to be accountable to anyone, never have to honor his marriage vows.

In effect, he had remained a kid. By disregarding the responsibilities associated with a truly mature adult, he could masquerade as a grown-up, but remain emotionally a child.

When our castle tumbled, when I could not process all that was happening in my life, I sought help. A kind, loving psychiatrist had an office just across the hall from Life Challenge. He was a gift from God.

At about the same time as our fall at PTL, other well-known evangelists' failures were exposed. It was alleged that one of them was consorting with prostitutes in a bizarre sexual manner. Of course, everyone was stunned. Was this a first-time experience for the high-profile preacher and singer? Because it was a subject of national attention, and it was known that I was his friend, I discovered his failure and shared my concerns with my doctor.

"You know, there's help for a person like that — I only wish he would let me help him," my doctor stated. "Sexual aberrations so often are a clear signal of a person not developing into adulthood. They got stuck in the adolescent sexual interests, and years later, their childhood sexual exploration goes on. They simply did not mature. I would do anything I could to have the opportunity to make sure there is help for him."

We have people seeking maturity in our Life Challenge office every day. He's a midwestern gentlemen, a California stockbroker, a rancher in Montana, or tends vineyards in Vermont. He's a man on the verge of annihilation because he never grew up.

Women are not exempt from this lack of maturity. She may be a machine technician, school teacher, a business woman, a homemaker, or an office worker. But she has one trait in common with her male counterpart — like him, she has never learned to submit to authority or developed the maturity that will make her adequate for life.

You can see the trauma caused by immaturity wherever you look. In fact, the most immature people are not always teenagers or young adults. An 86-year-old, great-grand-mother who taught Sunday school for decades can be immature. So can a middle-aged preacher. Anyone can struggle with immaturity, but the key is, how do we identify it and overcome the problem it creates?

Some traits or signs that will help you to identify the immature person are:

- They resist change.
- They are constantly restless or not settled in a job or relationship.
- They selfishly demand their own way.
- They have not fully developed their life and character.

Resisting Change

Resisting change can result from a selfish spirit.
A father refuses to attend church with his family be-

cause Sunday morning is the day he takes his boat out to the lake. Or, he may sleep in and then just putter around the house.

He may provide well financially for his family, but if he's not attending church and assuming responsibility and leading his family spiritually, he's immature. If he constantly protests that he needs more time to himself because of all this bread-winning, then he may need help.

Does he have a selfish and conditional love? He doesn't really desire to grow up.

It was devastating to their family. Ellen's words were laced with tears.

"He took some of his things and moved out — he no longer wants to see our children," she began. "We have two boys, eight and ten, but he doesn't care about them anymore. He wants to be alone. He doesn't even touch me. He says he has to take time for himself."

Ellen was unable to think, function, and understand her husband's conduct. She was desperately seeking help. My heart was broken. This family was wiped out and on the verge of collapse. Ellen was desperately trying to put their lives back together.

Perhaps you're a lady with a friend or relative who won't reconcile with you in a long-standing personal conflict. You've seen the error of your ways and attempt a meeting, asking her forgiveness and pledging a new commitment to the relationship.

Your friend or your sister refuses.

It is possible that this bitter woman has some type of nagging physical ailment. She could have a shaky marriage. These "other unresolved problems" could be a direct result of your feud, or they all may stem from her basic immaturity in relationships.

Whether she admits it to herself or not, this woman could be resistant to change. She doesn't want to change the basic nature that sours relationship after relationship.

Restless and Unsettled

Let us suppose the one you love has a restless nature. He or she can't seem to get settled, whether it be a job or a relationship.

A single mother sighs heavily when she comes home from work everyday and sees her 32-year-old son sitting at the kitchen table, staring into space. "Finding oneself" is a noble goal, but if a grown person is still fumbling in the dark, that is a signal of some trouble.

From the mother's perspective, it has become tiresome watching this child make halfhearted attempts at gaining some independence. She loves her son deeply, and part of loving a child is helping him or her make a way in the world.

This scene is played out everyday across America. It's a sign of immaturity. Either the person won't assume the discipline to grow up, or there is the feeling it *can't* be done.

This feeling of hopelessness only further frustrates the one who needs to grow up. In fact, it is frustrating for everyone involved.

Selfish and Demanding

A third sign that your loved one has a problem growing up involves a refusal to consider others' feelings. Demanding your own way in the majority of situations is destructive and definitely immature.

We think of a four year-old throwing a temper tantrum in a department store. After a few minutes of an embarrassing outburst, humiliated parents give in and buy the toy.

So it is with a person of any age demanding to always be the top priority. There's no real difference between that small child and an adult daughter who takes and takes from her parents. If we condone that behavior, we're still buying toys.

Some go beyond demands and become bullies. The

line between making demands and becoming a bully is very thin. Bullies are children who've never grown up. They will have what they want or else. When confronted, they usually turn and run. We must never give in to bullies.

It is interesting to note that this behavior has been around since the beginning of mankind's time here on earth. Take the example of Cain, son of Adam and Eve and history's first murderer.

Cain had all three traits of an immature person. He resisted change; God gave him ample time to modify his sacrificial offering, as we see in the fourth chapter of Genesis: "The Lord looked with favor on Abel and his offering, but on Cain and his offering he did not look with favor."

Cain experienced extreme restlessness because of God's disfavor and no doubt took to pouting behind a tree somewhere. Genesis tells us Cain's face was "downcast."

"If you do what is right, will you not be accepted?" God asked (Gen. 4:7).

Instead, Cain hardened his heart and his head and determined to continue his practice of providing God a sacrificial pile of vegetables and fruits. Cain demanded his own way!

Finally, Cain, the first son of the first parents, continued to resist change, whining that he would be a marked man wherever he went. We find no record of his repentance.

By the grace of God, Cain was able to live out his days in relative peace, even having Enoch for a son! Thus, the man who had introduced some of mankind's first sins fathered a child who grew to be so righteous that God took him home without the experience of physical death!

The Bible, however, doesn't tell us if Cain ever grew up emotionally or not.

Hopefully, your loved one's outcome will be more definite.

Taking the Risk

Now that we've identified three ways to tell if your loved one hasn't grown up, how can we go about helping? Let me suggest three ways:

> • Be willing to risk helping.
> • Learn to listen.
> • Comfort *and* challenge.

Many family members find themselves paralyzed when it comes to helping a loved one. A problem gradually lingers until years pass.

If, for instance, your son has a maturity problem, and he passes into adulthood, how much risk is involved in confronting him? Are you at physical risk? Is there a risk of alienating him? You must answer these questions and settle on a confrontation, if that is necessary.

Many parents consider that confronting a wayward child is too risky. It might result in hurt feelings. But what is the immaturity hurting? Chances are, more relationships will be destroyed by letting the immaturity remain unchecked.

Never tell someone you love them if you're not willing to confront them. I run that risk of confronting constantly.

I was asked by concerned friends to confront a 52-year-old child who never grew up spiritually, emotionally, or fiscally. He was still a babe. He was taking money that was not his. When I confronted him, I thought he was going to hit me; he drew back his hand. I did not back away.

I told him in a straight-forward manner that I was going to help him grow up. I made very tough demands of him. I insisted that he submit to someone, get his life together, pay his bills on time . . . or I would take action against him. I meant what I said.

Two years later, at a public meeting, to my total surprise, a shocked congregation watched as this man stood and told his story.

"Pastor Dortch helped make a man of me," he said, through tears. "I'm getting my life put together now. Pastor loved me enough to confront me with my problem."

Learning to Listen

Learning to listen sounds easy and obvious. It is obvious, but not always easy.

If you are disgusted about some of the immature situations your daughter has gotten into, you may try to show your disapproval by giving her the "silent treatment." Angry at her inattention to growing up, you decide to cap your anger and frustration by not saying anything to her.

She has nothing mature to say anyway, you may think.

Stop! Muster up all the understanding you can, sit down, and listen to her. See if she has anything to say that the two of you can agree on. At first, you might feel like the Tin Man in need of oil to get your mouth open enough to say, "Honey, I don't want our problems to come between us. Sit down and tell me what's on your mind." This is far better than sliding into a prolonged stalemate.

I must admit that my most unreasonable, foolish moments are those occasions when I'm not listening to my wife, Mildred. I've been ashamed of myself when I knew she was hurting, and I did not listen. One of the things my wife and my lawyer have taught me is to be quiet, listen, and then respond. Hopefully, I will respond with maturity, also.

Comforting and Challenging

Once you have shown your concern by listening, you are now ready to consider how you can provide comfort and put forth challenges.

A fine line exists between providing patient, moral support toward the immature and laying down challenges that they might be equipped to handle. You must be firm and compassionate at the same time.

If you have a son who simply has no thoughts of leaving home (and he's 35!), it might be a good idea to nudge him out of the nest by broaching the subject frequently. He'll get tired of hearing it and decide to do something on his own. You're not hurting this grown man by insisting he get his own place. If the situation becomes tense, or hurt feelings result, try applying a little old-fashioned humor: "Son, I have every confidence you'll do fine on your own. After all, the milk you've been drinking out of our refrigerator all these years has helped you develop a good mind and strong body!"

In today's world, every parent should consider that there is a possibility that drugs or other addictive behavior may be a problem. A child may linger for monetary support, to fulfill his desire to keep his habit. It is a real world we live in, and if one believes he or she is going to be an exception, they are living in Fantasy Land.

I'm confident that child you push out of the nest will experience great joy in finding his or her independence. You cared enough to let that child find personal joy.

Thousands of people find themselves in a reversed situation.

Your mother or father may lapse into a bit of childish immaturity after an illness or injury, sinking into noticeable self-pity. If you care enough to help them make their golden years as independent as possible, you will challenge them to participate in physical therapy or get regular exercise. Remember, it is sometimes easier to bring soup to the bed three times a day than to help with a rigorous exercise program.

Both of these situations call for enabling the person in question to become excited about the possibilities of their growing processes. Challenge them to look beyond their present condition to improving their mind and body.

As you can see, immaturity can strike anyone at anytime. No one is immune. We all know at least one person who has trouble growing up. The key is helping that loved one overcome this problem.

It is the basis for everything that comes afterward.

Conclusion

Immaturity is nothing new. Your child didn't invent it. The one you love didn't put a new twist on it. Since it is a problem we all share to one degree or another, we must approach each other in a loving way, seeking to guide and instruct.

Vince Lombardi was a great football coach because he instinctively knew how to deal with the personality of each player on his team. So, too, do we have the authority to offer solutions to immaturity. God has given us that authority, bonded by compassion.

The key is whether you love someone enough to free them from this problem.

2

Making Commitments

But your hearts must be fully committed to the Lord our God, to live by his decrees and obey his commands, as at this time.   1 Kings 8:61

The uplifting story of Dennis Byrd, the defensive lineman of the New York Jets paralyzed on the field in 1992, is never far from my mind when I think of commitment. Dennis had all the fears and anxieties one would expect with a spinal injury. But, when the odds were against him, he made a commitment to walk again and share the miracle with the world. Commitment means a lot to Dennis Byrd.

In the troubled times in which we live, we must have an anchor. We need an anchor for our emotions and our physical needs. What is this anchor?

Commitment.

It is very popular nowadays, even common, to attempt

to wriggle out of relationships by saying, "I'm not into commitment."

Well, we'd better get into it, or there will be no substance to our lives. We must understand that commitment is essential. To paraphrase the commercial, it is "the fabric of our lives."

Commitment is one of those words that is used quite often, but it really doesn't mean much to a lot of people. Changing that attitude will do much to strengthen all aspects of our lives. Not keeping commitments takes away from our sense of well-being.

Recently, I received a phone call "live" on the air at 1:30 a.m.

The 17-year-old girl on the other end of the line said, "I had to leave my house to call you from a pay phone because my stepfather wouldn't let me use the phone."

I sensed her pain as she explained her predicament, "I am eight months pregnant by my 22-year-old boyfriend. Oh, he told me he would marry me. First it was in one month, then two months, then three months. Now the baby is almost due, and I have no way of supporting myself."

It's not an unusual story. A young man who fathers children at the drop of a hat hits the road once he finds out a baby is on the way. He refuses to make a commitment for a stable life, and now at least two lives will suffer because of cowardly selfishness.

Identifying the Uncommitted

How do you tell if your loved one has a problem with commitment?

- They are evasive and won't communicate.
- They have another agenda.
- They rarely keep their word.
- They are selfish.

You would be surprised at the number of people who have trouble discerning if their loved ones are shying away from commitments. The girl who is running after the father of her child as he is running away — she can be fairly sure he won't make a commitment, but she might debate the issue in her mind for months or years.

Some close themselves off to family and friends, refusing to communicate with those closest to them. Others are so transparent in their hollow commitments, you can be fairly sure they will bail out when the commitment no longer suits them. This goes right into not keeping our word.

Judas made a commitment to Christ early on, but the lure of money caused him to hide his new agenda — until the soldiers arrived with their swords drawn in the Garden of Gethsemane. Jesus loved Judas, but the flawed follower allowed his lack of commitment to become history's most famous betrayal. The love of God's own Son wasn't enough to prevent disaster for the infamous Apostle.

Family Commitments

When I make a commitment to my wife for life, a sense of order and security is immediately established, which is essential for trust in the marriage. The ones we love have the right to expect that we are going to make commitments, and we have the right to expect commitments on their part. This has to do with our basic root values of life.

Society abounds with broken lives destroyed by lack of commitment. It never surprises me to learn that the famous couple who two years before signed "pre-nuptial agreements" to protect their own assets are now signing divorce papers. Two people who can't commit their possessions to the one they supposedly "love" surely can't commit their fidelity, their loyalty, or the rest of their lives.

Without commitment from both husband and wife, a marriage is doomed from the "I do."

Commitment affects not only marriage, but every aspect of family life. To make my point, let me ask you: Do you keep your word?

If you make a commitment to take your son fishing, you'd better be setting a worm on that hook come Saturday morning. If you make a commitment to mete out some kind of discipline, you need to carry out the punishment without wavering. Children become what we teach them.

If you consistently break your promises or back off on following through with a forewarned discipline, then your children will learn that you can't be trusted. Imagine the insecurity that sets up in a child's mind.

Some kids are outspoken about a parent's inability to keep their word. How many times have you heard a child angrily say, "You broke your promise! You always say you're going to take me to the movies, but you never do!"

Broken promises lead to broken hearts, and broken hearts can lead to broken lives down the road. Be faithful to keep your word to your children and your spouse.

Committed to Church and Work

Commitment is needed in all areas of our lives.

We must make a commitment to our church. "Forsake not the assembling of yourselves together" (Heb. 10:25). God didn't create discipline as a hobby; it must be put into practice.

Millions of people have a cavalier attitude toward church: "If it suits me, and it's not raining or too hot or too cold, and I don't have any other plans, then . . . maybe I'll drag myself out of bed and go to church."

Jesus left the splendor of heaven to come down to this miserable planet to spill His blood on a rough, tortuous cross one cold and rainy day. I'm so glad He didn't say, "I'll do it if it suits Me."

Surely we can "take up our cross" and get out of our warm, soft beds to sit in padded, air-conditioned comfort for an hour or so on Sunday morning. Surely we can find it within our hearts to take a few moments to show our appreciation and praise for the Saviour who laid down His life for our sins. Surely we can commit ourselves to serving our brothers and sisters in Christ without envy or resentment but out of love and humility. Is that asking too much? God is expecting something in return for His investment in us.

As Christians, it is our "duty" to attend a Bible-believing church regularly, to participate in church activities, to tithe, and to pray for our church leaders. To do anything less borders on rebellion to God who ordained the church as the "body of Christ." We cannot call ourselves Christians and not be involved with other believers in a church where Jesus is preached and our Creator is worshipped.

Let me also stress the importance of commitment to one body of believers. I know of Christians who hop from one church to another in an effort to find the perfect pastor, a loving congregation, and a growing Sunday school. Yet, these same people refuse to become members of the church, do not tithe, and grumble and complain when things don't go their way. At the first oversight or slightest personal affront, they are out the door and down the street to the next church.

Commitment means praying for the pastor and his spiritual growth; becoming an active member who is willing to wash dishes after the church picnic; teaching Sunday school to sniveling two year olds; taking meals to the sick; and giving one-tenth of your income to support the ministries of the church. In most congregations, 20 percent of the people do 100 percent of the work to keep the church functioning and ministering to the other 80 percent.

We learn that when we work together, making commitments to one another, we are then able to commit to a larger group and to ourselves. Don't expect it to be easy to make commitments . . . but they are worth it.

What about the workplace? Are you committed to being on time, putting in a full day's work, and doing your job without grumbling or complaining? When we make commitments to carry out our responsibilities at work, it affects everyone around us and can only bring about positive results — both for you and your boss.

I have had to make many decisions about people in the workplace. I've had 2,000 people under my direct leadership. The person who is faithful, who serves diligently, is the one I want to work with. They will, over time, achieve what others can't. My experience is, the clever come and go. The dependable endure.

The results of keeping commitments become apparent very quickly in our lives. If we are committed to our spouses, our children, our employers, and our church, then our lives exhibit a harmony that keeps every area in perfect order.

Helping the Uncommitted

How do you help a loved one make commitments?

- Commit and submit yourself.
- Set an example of commitment.
- Demonstrate the results of commitment.

First, you become part of the commitment yourself. We must meet people halfway. When we become part of the commitment process, it is easier to get the other person to do it.

Perhaps you need to sit down with your spouse and verbally reaffirm your commitment to him or her. If you are a wife, read the New Testament Scriptures dealing with God's expectations of you. Then, lovingly express to your husband your willingness to submit to him, to honor him, to respect him, and to be faithful to him. Expect nothing at this time from your husband, but commit yourself to being the kind of wife God wants you to be.

Not long after she was married, a young woman gave her life to Christ. Her husband, who was raised in a tradi-tional denomination, refused to attend the full-gospel, independent church where she had recently been baptized as a believer.

At first, she nagged and begged him to join her, but to no avail. "I don't feel comfortable with that style of worship," he told her firmly.

On the advice of friends, she began to fast and pray diligently for her husband's salvation.

"I would like for us to attend church together," she said sweetly. "On Sundays, I will go with you to the early service at your church." Afterward, she drove herself to the full-gospel church for the later service and returned in time for them to lunch together. This continued for several years.

During this time, she interceded regularly for her husband and asked others to pray for him but seldom suggested that he attend church with her. At times he did go to special drama presentations or musicals.

After a while, her silent witness of faith began to melt his stubborn heart. She noticed he was reading the Bible every day and that a dramatic change had taken place in his personality.

One Sunday, he overslept, and it was too late to attend the early service at his church. "Let's just go to your church today," he said, smiling and caressing her hand.

From that day on, they went to the church together, where they have both continued to grow in the Lord. Husbands must give some kind of commitment to their wives.

Set an Example

Secondly, you may need to set an example of true commitment. As you begin to exhibit commitment in your marriage, your spouse will feel more secure in the relationship and hopefully begin to respond with renewed commitment on their part.

The evidence of commitment is seen in the little things of life. If your spouse asks you to take the suits to the cleaners on Monday, do it if at all possible. If he likes gravy with his mashed potatoes, make it for him without complaining. If she likes to take a nap on Sunday afternoon, keep the kids quiet for an hour or so.

Then when it comes time for you to ask for a favor, your loved one will be more willing to respond. This may take time, but there is nothing more powerful in a marriage than loving submission to one another in the little things over a period of time.

Of course, if you're dealing with a friend, father, or aunt who has a problem keeping commitments, you will change the scenario. Submission doesn't just involve marriage partners, but Scripture tells us, "Submit to one another out of reverence for Christ" (Eph. 5:21). That means *you* must be willing to set the example and go out of your way or get your hands dirty in order to be faithful to them.

I know what you are thinking: *What if they try to take advantage of my submissive attitude?*

My advice is: Don't give up right away. Keep it up, but at the same time begin to expect something from them in return. This is not your motive, of course, but your desire is for them to learn commitment. And the best way for them to learn is to practice it.

Never assume that the one you love understands what you mean by a commitment. Their background might have been such that they have never experienced or lived-out what true commitment is. Sometimes you have to show people and express to them that commitment means keeping your word. They might have come from an environment where people told them pretty much whatever they wanted them to hear.

Demonstrate the Results

We must demonstrate the results of a commitment and provide a glimpse of the rewards of an unselfish act. Give your uncommitted loved one an example of you keeping commitments in your home. He or she will want to be a part of that, and it will snowball.

When I went through the greatest heartbreaks of my life, it was most rewarding for me to experience the faithfulness of our children in helping my wife and I. The commitment of our children to us as their parents was a genuine blessing.

There were occasions when both Deanna and Rich had definite guidance for both Mildred and me. All of our commitments were enriched and confirmed during these troubled times.

The day came in my life when I was so overwhelmed with my problems and needs that our son came to me and said, "Dad, I love you so much that I have to tell you something. You have built your whole life on being perceptive and being smart enough to know what to do. You have built a life and a career out of making good decisions. With the stress that you are now under, your judgment is being affected. For a while, let me make your decisions until you regain your balance."

One of the smartest things I've ever done was to say, "Rich, you're right. I will do that."

At that moment, I saw the fruit of over 30 years of my fatherly commitment to raising godly, mature children. Our children let us know that we mattered as parents and as individuals. If you want your children to be committed to you later in life, you must be committed to them early on.

With springtime in the air, a father signed up his son for little league baseball at their local community center. Although the boy had not played the game for several years, they both thought this would be a good opportunity for him to develop new skills and learn to be part of a team.

During practice sessions, the coach encouraged the newcomer, who was tall and strong for his age. Expecting him to be a big hitter, he worked on batting practice and outfielding.

When the games started, the coach put the new kid up to bat, hoping for a home run. Instead, the rookie pitcher on the other team threw a wild pitch hitting the batter in the face. Trying to hide his pain, the newcomer took his base — but lost his confidence.

The father watched and prayed, hoping his son would be able to regain his assurance and perform.

As the season went on, however, the boy continued to disappoint his coaches, his team, and himself. With every mistake, one of the coaches would scream in the boy's face, "What's the matter with you? Can't you do anything right?"

Soon, the boy was spending most of every game sitting on the bench.

One night after a game, the teen came home and said, "The coach said anyone who's not interested in playing should quit. I think he meant me."

Outraged, his father called the coach who further criticized the boy for his lack of performance. "He's a liability to the team." Angry at the treatment his boy had received at the hands of this insensitive coach whose only goal was winning at any cost, the father didn't know what to do.

"Son," he said, realizing his child's self-esteem was at stake, "you gave it your best. I'm very proud of you, but I will not let you continue to be harassed by this coach."

Then, to save the boy's pride, the father made the decision, "I don't want you to play on that team any longer. I love you too much to subject you to that kind of verbal abuse."

Although the boy was disappointed, he learned an important lesson that day: Dad was committed to what was best for him as his son. It didn't matter what other people thought or said, Dad was on his side.

Conclusion

At the end of the journey, we will never be disappointed by the commitments we have made — if we keep our eyes on the Lord. The ultimate commitment we make is when we make a commitment of ourselves to God. He made a commitment to us when He sent His Son to hang on a rough cross.

That's what makes our journey complete.

Commitment is one of the things that sets us apart from the rest of creation. We have the capacity to be loyal to each other, although that seems in short supply today. Commitment endures over the decades, through grief, happiness, hardship. All of it.

Our greatest example of commitment comes from our Father. He made a decision to save us from sin and has promised that His commitment will stand the tests of time and hell. The devil may try to fool us into thinking commitment is hollow from the top on down, but we know differently through the grace of our Lord Jesus.

Start with that, expand it to your relationships, and the ones you love will follow suit. Believe it.

3

Relationships

Live in harmony with one another. Do not be
proud, but be willing to associate with people. . . .
Rom. 12:16

When I became a foreign missionary, I came before one of the most righteous men I've ever met. Noel Perkins was director of the division of foreign missions for my denomination — a noble person whose unblemished character was an inspiration to us all. My destiny was in his hands as I presented myself for consideration as a foreign missionary.

When he looked at me so compassionately and asked what I felt I needed as a foreign missionary, I responded that I needed more Bible study and prayer. He kindly looked at me and said, "Probably your greatest asset will be your ability to work with others on a foreign field. Your relationships with them will be your most important task."

He knew that being away from home and raising a family would be a challenge, and his words taught me one of the great lessons of my life.

As Christians, we need a passion for friendships and relationships that matter. They are so important. Relationships are eternal. If you can't manage and maintain relationships, you cannot function in this world.

While I was involved at PTL, the people who meant the most to me had taken secondary roles in my life. I put them there because I was more engaged in my work and in fulfilling a dream than I was in people. Well, the dream vanished, and the people I loved the most were on the outside. The dream shattered because I was too involved in what was best for Richard Dortch. I no longer listened to friends.

My dearest friend since college days, Daniel Johnson, said to me one day when I was at my so-called peak, "You know, I almost never see you anymore." He was trying to reach me, and I was so intoxicated with myself, I couldn't respond.

Friends reached out and tried to help me, but I was so enamored with what I wanted to do.

You can tell someone you love has a problem with relationships when their fixation is on something that will fade away. That's why it is good to keep an eternal perspective on everything we do. All that we see with our eyes will someday be gone, but relationships are eternal.

When we get to heaven, it won't matter that you were the top ad salesman in your department from 1979-86. What will matter is if the co-worker you had a chance to help is standing next to you. That relationship is eternal.

Relationships are among the most critical areas of our lives. For some, however, it is more important to spread hideous, crippling lies than it is to make a right relationship. So relationships aren't just ignored; sometimes they are abused and trampled.

Relationships are *eternal*. That means relationships are going to go on.

Family relationships are holy. One of the tragedies of life today is the breach of relationships between members of families. It used to be that a family was in the geographical range of an hour's journey; in today's society, it is so easy to get pulled apart from our families.

I recently heard Billy Graham interviewed on "Larry King Live," and he said his biggest failure in life was that he spent more time in his ministry than he did with his family. He regretted that. If a righteous man like Billy Graham can make that confession, what does it say about the rest of us?

How many of us have broken relationships with close family members? Children only see their fathers once or twice and it fades away.

One day recently, I was talking to a man who has professional input into our ministry. I told him, "I want to write about the importance of relationships."

I had barely gotten the words out of my mouth when this successful consultant looked across the table at Mildred and me and began to cry.

Stunned, we sat in silence watching this huge man sob.

I knew the best thing to do was remain quiet, and finally he said, "I have not seen my father for over 17 years. I have tried to contact him in another part of the country, but he won't talk to me. I have no relationship with him. He will not accept my calls. A piece of my life is missing."

A piece of my life is missing.

God help us to repair this kind of damage!

Unmasking the Unrelated

If a loved one has a problem with relationships, it may be masking itself in other ways. Or you may be already aware of how it is affecting their life, but you may not realize the depth of its effects.

There are so many ways to tell if a loved one is having trouble in relationships, but let's look at three:

- They become self-centered.

- They lose a sense of passion about friendships.
- They become exclusive — shutting down relationships and friendships.

We've all met people who have a problem with sharing themselves. If a self-centered person has ever made headway in a relationship, it quickly is eroded by an obsession with "me." More often than not, the self-absorbed person never gets to first base in a relationship.

Here is an interesting aspect to this problem. It is good for us to actually nurture a little bit of self-interest. For instance, it is important to get your loved one to a point where he or she says, "I'm going through a problem, and I need you as a friend. I don't need your money, or your advice . . . I need you. I need the presence of your friendship."

I have had the unusual experience over the years to have a warm relationship with every pastor my home church has had. During the days of my heartbreaking experience, God was kind enough to let us have the Rev. Dale Edwards as our pastor. Through my loneliness and despair, the day came when I said to him, "I need your love and affirmation in my life. What you are and what you personally represent means so much to me, and I draw strength from you."

That is a good expression of need. It is only when the emphasis is *always* on me that it becomes a problem.

A second warning sign is when a person loses a sense of passion about friendships. This can either signal added troubles like the hint of depression that could lead to some kind of self-abuse, or it can merely mean the one you love has become interested in *things*. You want to monitor when the person exhibits this behavior because they take on a certain kind of loneliness that is abnormal.

You can tell if there is a problem with relationships when a person becomes exclusive. When they don't broaden their outreach, somebody might influence them to withhold their friendship from others and just give their attention to them.

Helping to Heal Broken Relationships

How do we turn these problems around and direct our loved ones toward finding peace with God and help for themselves?

- Confront the loved one with our expectations.
- Get involved with the loved one and his interests.
- Find a common ground.
- Ask a third party to mediate.

For one thing, we must confront the loved one and tell them what our expectations are. Don't be afraid to do this.

A wife must tell her husband that she considers their relationship to be a top priority, and that they need to spend quality time together every week. Tell the man you married that you want to be his sweetheart, his lover, his friend. Impress on him that this is a small price to pay to keep the relationship intact.

A young pastor who was engaged to be married suddenly found himself "falling out of love" with his fiancée. Troubled by this development and knowing that his reputation and ministry hung in the balance, he went to an older man for advice.

"Start acting like you love her," the wise elder instructed.

"How do I do that when I don't feel like it?" the young pastor asked.

"You just do it, and the feelings will come," he said. "Remember, love is something you do."

After receiving this advice, the young man went straight to the florist shop and ordered a dozen roses to be sent to his fiancée. Then he made a resolution to phone her every day until the wedding and tell her he loved her. While driving in the car together, he would force himself to take her hand and kiss her good night at the end of the evening.

The week before the wedding, he saw the older man at church. "How's it going?" the elder asked.

"I can't believe it!" the young pastor exclaimed. "I love her more now than I did when we first met. I can't wait for our wedding day!"

Next, if you're troubled about someone who has lost a passion for friendships, pick out the things she or he is focusing on and analyze the situation. Don't jump into criticizing right off the bat. Ask yourself a few questions and decide if taking an interest in this loved one's hobbies or obsessions will help get rid of the behavior.

A young man watched his beloved go off to college while he stayed behind to work the farm. While on campus, she wrote letters telling of her discoveries in literature and drama. "I've found a whole new world," she wrote. The letters, however, became fewer and further between.

Heavy-hearted, the young farmer went to his pastor for advice. "If these things are benefiting her as a person, she should be encouraged to pursue them," the clergyman suggested. "But if her personality changes and she begins to drift away, trouble may be brewing."

"What should I do?" the young man asked.

"Before she comes home for the holidays," the pastor advised, "purchase tickets to a play in the city. Find out everything you can about the actors and the story, and show her you are interested in learning more about this new world of drama."

"Do you think that will help?" the farmer wondered aloud.

"If you try to stifle her newfound expressions," the wise man replied, "most likely you will push her away. If you can share in her interests, the passion might return to her heart."

"Well, I'll give it a try," the young man responded.

"One more piece of advice," the pastor continued, "tell her how much you care and how much you want your relationship to continue. But don't demand that she change or respond irrationally to her interest in other things. Give her time and space, and if she truly loves you, her feelings will once again be ignited."

The young farmer did as the pastor instructed, and by New Year's Day, the couple was engaged.

"How did you do it?" the pastor asked when he learned the news.

"I told her I'd convert that old unused barn into a theater and start a community drama group," the farmer said with a twinkle in his eye.

Talk about finding a common ground!

Common Ground and Mediators

Sometimes, the person who has become exclusive about relationships is harder to deal with because many times one or more people are on the other side, vying for the attentions of your loved one.

A new wife may find herself in competition with her new mother-in-law, or a husband may be up against two sisters-in-law who refuse to share their sister — his wife. A furious or irrational response by the husband will make it easy to predict where the problem is headed.

That man needs to step back and do a little reasoning. If the husband says to the sisters-in-law, "Here's what I'm willing to do to enhance the relationship," the emotional ammunition that could be used against him is now of no use. Probably, this will catch the sisters-in-law off guard, and he will come away a hero in his wife's eyes.

One of the ways to heal these gaps is to find a mutual friend, a pastor, or a leader whom both partners respect. Let the third party act as the referee who listens to both sides and assesses the situation. After making suggestions, he then can encourage the two parties to act upon his advice.

That scenario could be applied to any relationship where one party has become exclusive. Those involved must be willing to act upon the advice given and realize that if the relationship matters, time and effort are key ingredients.

Conclusion

We can all accumulate things. We can buy almost anything we want in our society. We can hoard. But without relationships, we live empty lives and die alone.

You don't want that, do you? You don't want it for yourself, or for the one you love.

When God had created a perfect earth, and brought a man out of the dust, He gifted Adam with that most precious thing, a relationship. He gave him Eve.

And so it is today, as we go through our individual lives and days. We must maintain and protect this gift from God, the relationship, for it makes us whole and happy, content and at peace.

4

Honesty

Truthful lips endure forever, but a lying tongue lasts only a moment.   Prov. 12:19

Arthur Newington was a sainted evangelical leader in Great Britain. As a young man I sat spellbound and listened to the remarkable stories he recounted. I was fortunate to have him as a friend.

In the early part of this century the most well-known and unusual minister both in the USA and around the world was an apostolic figure named Smith Wigglesworth.

Wigglesworth frequently came as a guest minister at the church where the Newingtons served as pastors. These were the World War II years. Almost every thing was rationed in England — food, clothing — all the necessities of life.

Mrs. Newington noticed that their guest, Wigglesworth, relished the coffee she served. At that time, coffee was a high priority, tightly rationed item. Mr. Wigglesworth would drink it slowly, enjoying every sip with great pleasure. The gracious hostess was so impressed by her guest's appreciation for the coffee that she decided to serve it often.

When Wigglesworth's visit was finished, his clothes packed, and he was on his way out of the house, Mrs. Newington stopped this righteous man and handed him a glass jar wrapped in a paper sack.

Wigglesworth abruptly stopped and asked what was in the jar. "It is the coffee," she said. "I wanted you to have what we have left."

"I could never take it." Wigglesworth replied. "I have coveted that coffee since I have been here. I must not take it. It would be wrong."

That is honesty at its basic level.

"To thine own self be true," Shakespeare said. When we are honest with ourselves, it is the norm to be honest with others — and with God.

John the apostle reminds us that as long as "we walk in the light, we have fellowship with one another" (1 John 1:7). If we protest that we have done nothing wrong, "the truth is not in us."

This is a very powerful and sobering statement.

We must not focus only on the consequences of dishonesty. Rather, we should focus on what walking in the light can do for us and our relationships.

Honesty vs. *Dishonesty*

When we are honest and conduct our relationships in that way, life is significantly more rich and beautiful. The air smells fresher, food tastes better, and people enjoy our company. How long has it been since you ate a delicious meal and sat on your porch inhaling the sweet night air? You were free, there was nothing hidden in your life. You were in perfect peace.

Only those who practice honesty can live in a state of harmony with themselves, others, and their Creator. It is only then that we are able to see the glory and majesty of God.

Honesty of heart and mind is critical to our relationship with God. He cannot look upon evil. It is Satan who is the father of lies. As the sands of time become fewer in number, this deceiver seeks to mold humanity in his wicked image. As a result, life is teeming with people who lie.

Those who make a habit of practicing dishonesty fail to learn that God is most fair in His judging of mankind. Those who genuinely seek Him, however, find supernatural freedom. The honest person is unchained.

What about the person who is embezzling from his company or having an affair with a co-worker or fudging on his income tax forms? He wakes up each morning, having slept little all night. During the day, the stress of covering up his dishonesty and the constant thought of being discovered puts him under extreme duress.

Dishonest people fail to realize that at the root of their misery is guilt brought on by the practice of dishonesty.

If you are waking up each morning with stress of the soul, you need to evaluate the level of honesty and integrity in your life. Mental and physical suffering is often the result of not following the path of honesty.

Notice how chillingly thorough King David was in his dishonest and murderous dealings with Uriah the Hittite, husband of Bathsheba. If you read 2 Samuel, chapter 11, David's frustration with Uriah grew out of the soldier's almost cartoonish loyalty to the king.

David had already gone far past wrestling with his own conscience where Bathsheba was concerned. After he had committed adultery with Uriah's beautiful and available wife, David first tried to convince Uriah to go home, hoping the warrior would have relations with his wife and cover the pregnancy David knew existed. The king suggested R & R. When Uriah refused to enjoy comforts that his own men could not, an exasperated David got him drunk and nudged him toward home. The next morning, Uriah was found sleeping on a mat with the king's servants!

Finally, in acute frustration, David ordered Uriah to be put on the front lines in the siege of Jerusalem. Sure enough, that did the trick, and Uriah died. Now David was free to marry Bathsheba, and he did, but oh, how he suffered for it. The baby's death was only the beginning of the trail of heartache that would follow David throughout the remainder of his life.

If one of the greatest men in history was capable of this kind of cold, calculated lying, what does it say for the rest of us? Lying, and the covering of lies, is an all-consuming thing. It destroys trust in relationships, and it eventually kills the things most important to us.

The Practicing Deceiver

If you are worried about a loved one who has gotten into trouble over dishonest practices — or if trouble looms — there are definite warning signs.

- They deceive themselves and others.
- They fail to speak up when something is wrong.
- Open, one-on-one communication disappears.
- They will avoid serious discussions at all costs.

Children, who are much more transparent than adults, exhibit these same traits when they are trying to hide the truth. Although grown-ups are much more sophisticated, the way children respond reflects how most adults react. Does this scenario sound familiar?

The sweet child who yesterday offered you hugs and kisses now avoids your eyes when talking to you. He stops telling you what is going on at school or in the neighborhood and gives curt yes and no answers. Sensing something is wrong, you question him, trying to get to the heart of the matter. Threatened by your intrusion and fear of discovery, he lies to cover up.

Fortunately, most children don't lie very well and seldom dispose of damaging evidence. Soon you realize his stories don't add up, bringing you to the point of insistent interrogation. Like your local police or the FBI, parents learn what kinds of questions to ask, and the case is easily solved.

If, however, swift and effective punishment is not administered, children will learn that lying brings minimal discomfort and few consequences. Adults who have learned to lie as children won't stop just because they are older. The cycle continues, once those who lie become parents. They are less likely to discipline their own children when it comes to not telling the truth.

If your spouse makes light of your child's dishonest acts, that may be a sign that his own life is less than one of complete integrity.

Deceived and Deceiving

When I confronted an outstanding businessman who was being unfaithful to his wife, his disclaimer was, "I've never been more successful than I am now."

A person who is dishonest must convince himself or herself that what is being done has some justification.

Once the lying to self is achieved, it's a piece of cake to lie to others. If you can lie to yourself, lying to anyone — even those you love — becomes natural.

Silent Agreement

When you fail to speak up, it's an obvious fact that you are protecting your own position and you are more concerned about yourself than the events that are occuring around you. I suffered a tremendous loss in my life because

I failed to speak up. I knew I was leaving an impression that brought people to false conclusions.

Had I spoken up and been honest, perhaps there could have been a different consequence. I've always felt that I was severely punished for what I didn't do, rather than any wrongful participation and evil. It's easy to get sucked into things. It won't make any difference whether the truth comes out, but take it from someone who's paid a high price — we must get the truth out, and the sooner the better.

Silence can be wrong. Silence can be a shadowy confederate of lying, because refusal to speak up in wrong situations is never a gray area. If you know you are participating in a lie that hurts someone else and benefits you, that is as wrong as if the lie came out of your mouth. *A lie can come out of a closed mouth.*

That can lead to a whole host of other consequences, by the way. Just ask someone who's lost everything through dishonesty.

Broken Lines of Communication

Other factors can contribute to dishonesty, but if you suspect this is the problem, a sure warning sign is the withdrawal of your loved one. If your loved one is being dishonest, he or she will stop talking to you.

How well I know how smooth some people can be, acting as if nothing is wrong. However, there is a lack of transparency; it will show at some level. When the one you love seems too accommodating, too nice, that can mean very deep and perverse hidden sins. When George became overly-interested in me and my well-being, and wanted to help me in so many of my tasks, I was very pleased and somewhat overwhelmed by his kindness. He just couldn't do enough for us. Several months later, I knew why. His participation in a most despicable sexual sin had come to light and he knew all along that I would be one of the people sitting in judgment of him.

Your husband might snap at you for any reason at all. That's his own guilt reaction. True communication will be yesterday's news.

Your nephew, with whom you've always been close, suddenly becomes sullen and detached. That's because he stole money from you, without your being aware of it.

Once, I was stunned when shaking hands with some very kind people when a gentleman said to me, "Why did William steal my wife? He has ruined me, my family, and everything that I've always believed."

He was talking about a person who was my friend, who had had a severe moral failure.

"I trusted him so much — can I ever believe in him again?"

Those are sobering words.

Helping the Lying Loved One

How can you help a loved one overcome a problem with lying? This is another area that requires something of you — the one doing the helping.

- Forgive the dishonest person.
- Let your life be an example of honesty.
- Give him the gift of loyalty.
- Tell him how to receive God's forgiveness.
- Trust him, but insist on accountability and submission.

First, you must forgive, especially if you are the victim of lies. Do you have any idea of the marvelous release you can bring to a person if you meet them at the door with forgiveness? Watch that moody and withdrawn spirit melt away. It will bring freedom for the one who feels he is condemned to a life of deceit.

Forgiveness is not always pleasant, but it is also not optional. We are commanded to forgive. All of us have lied at one time or another. Put yourself in the place of the one doing the lying. Did you not feel a weight lift off your shoulders when *you* were forgiven?

Next, use your own life as an example of the benefits that walking in the light of God can bring. Believe me, your honest personality will make an impact on those around you.

The apostle John made no impossible demands on us when he spoke of walking in the light. He was a human, too, and understood that none of us are perfect. But he did demand that we should, in all sincerity, place ourselves under the influence of the light which is in God. He implored us to keep striving with zeal to pattern ourselves after God.

What an impact it will have on your loved one if you first provide this kind of example, then explain the benefits and joys associated with it. Would the one you love not want to trade those hurts and fearful life for one of peace and joy? Help the ones you love to achieve this.

Challenge them to see the rewards of their efforts at practicing honesty. Give them a glimpse of a clean future.

Another way to help a loved one with an honesty problem is give them the gift of loyalty. Your unconditional loyalty will serve as a crucial model for those whose lives are steeped in deceit and dirty dealings. If you can show a troubled loved one that they will not be condemned and exposed — at least by you — they will have at least a faint glimmer of hope that they can shed the old skin and begin walking upright in honesty.

We must give people hope and when our love translates to action, it gives us a new and meaningful life.

When I was out of circulation and became a symbol of public shame, my dear friends Karl and Joyce Strader contacted both Mildred and I every other week for 16 months, and shared their love with us. When I would attempt to put myself down and sometimes overstate my failure, these friends were a great source of encouragement because of their loyalty.

Remember, we are all family when we have participated in God's love.

Roy Rogers was once commenting on some of the dilemmas of life. This wonderful man, who along with his lovely wife, Dale Evans, has championed Christian values in Hollywood films, had some profound advice for those caught in some moral problem. This cowboy actor said, "It might hurt to do the right thing, but afterwards, you'll feel better."

How simple yet profound! What a release that statement should be for one struggling in the mud of dishonesty. Tell that to your loved one.

Jesus Christ hung on a cross and felt the weight of every lie ever told, from every person in every walk of life, and from every time period in history. He knew our sins intimately, and they brought sweat drops of blood. He suffered for us all and made sure that no lie has to keep any of us from the Father.

Challenge your loved ones to be honest with God. Tell them that the admission of their sins will cleanse their souls and free them from the bondage of guilt and shame. "If we confess our sin, he is faithful and just and will forgive our sin and cleanse us from all unrighteousness" (1 John 1:9).

When I was in prison, one of my fellow inmates was crushed at the realization of what his failures had done to him and the ones he loved. I shared with him a poem, written by an author whose name I do not know:

> As I walked through the woodland meadows
> Where sweetly the thrushes sing,
> I found on a bed of mosses
> A bird with a broken wing.
> I healed his hurt each morning
> And he sang the sweet refrain,
> But the bird with the broken pinion
> Never soared as high again.

A young life by sin is smitten
With all its seductive art,
And moved with Christ-like pity
I took him to my heart.
He lived with noble purpose,
He struggled not in vain,
But the bird with the broken pinion
Never soared as high again.

A broken friend added another verse:

The life that sin has smitten
With all of its guilt and its stain,
By the grace and merit of Jesus
CAN soar as high again!

Conclusion

The sin of lying is one of the most difficult to pry loose. It cements itself around all aspects of our lives and finally so clouds our reality that we become different people.

But it doesn't have to remain.

We can take anything to the Lord in prayer, either for ourselves or for the ones we love. God can conquer our lying. He can make us new creatures. It doesn't matter if you are a respected member of the community, or one who stays behind the scenes. God hears us all. Confess your dishonest nature to Him in a sincere way, and let Him energize your life. You will be transformed. You will be whole.

5

Discipline

My son, do not make light of the Lord's discipline, and do not lose heart when he rebukes you, because the Lord disciplines those he loves, and he punishes everyone he accepts as a son.

Heb. 12:15-16

When we think of discipline, we often think of children, but discipline encompasses many things. It is not always something we dispense, but rather, it is something we grow into and maintain.

God has promised to be with us in our personal lives — if we obey Him. That is His pledge to us as individuals, and obeying Him is our response to His love. Obedience is also the cornerstone of discipline. Some people, however, have trouble summoning up enough responsibility to manifest this discipline of obedience in their lives.

We must obey Him! If we adhere to that principle, we will rarely find ourselves in a discipline problem.

Sadly, however, scores of people in today's society could list discipline as their number one problem. Some can't discipline themselves to balance a checkbook. Others see no need in attending church regularly. There are all kinds of examples of people with weak discipline.

When a businessman friend was asked why he was certifying and documenting every product that he made, when there was "no way" anyone could ever know, he responded quicky, "I know it, and I won't cheat. As long as I know it, I won't do it — I'll never take a shortcut."

You cannot come to a place of discipline in your life without a relationship with God. It is beyond necessary. God almighty is desiring every one of us to develop Christian character so that others will see Jesus in us. God wants to bring us to the place where, like the apostle Paul, we can say, "I live, yet not I, but Christ liveth in me" (Gal. 2:20). That is the discipline we should strive for.

Two Kinds of Discipline

There are several kinds of discipline. The Lord disciplined me for not seeking first the Kingdom and His righteousness. Here are two points to ponder:

1) We can discipline ourselves by submitting to others. That is judging ourselves.
2) We will come under God's discipline if we do not discipline ourselves.

Traits of the Undisciplined

You may think that this kind of spiritual advice isn't going to do much good in the situation you are dealing with. Oh? And where do you want to start with your loved one who has lost his or her grip on discipline?

Discipline goes hand-in-hand with a close relationship with the Father. If you keep that in mind when trying to help a loved one lacking in discipline, you won't feel such an overwhelming burden, nor will the loved one feel pressured to change.

First, let's determine if maintaining discipline is your loved one's basic problem. There are three obvious ways to identify those who are undisciplined:

- Key areas of their life are falling apart — finances, education, job.
- They procrastinate and refuse to get things done.
- They fail to have priorities and a sense of purpose.

Don't always assume that a discipline problem will crop up right in front of your nose. Your loved one may be exhibiting erratic behavior, and you won't be able to pinpoint a lack of discipline right away. You'll have to wait for a problem to reveal itself in a big way.

You'd be surprised how many people can cover financial problems until they reach gargantuan proportions. Perhaps your husband has been evasive about the family's financial situation. He can carry this off only so long as the creditors don't call or write. It's conceivable this situation can go on for years and starts with not paying bills on time. The consequences can be shattering.

Or suppose your boss is also your sister who takes a ho-hum attitude toward her business. This directly affects your living situation. Her lack of discipline in business dealings is running the company into bankruptcy and threatening your job security.

What about the son who lets his college attendance slip to the point where he is put on academic probation? That is a problem you might not have seen coming until it's too late. Where did it start? Maybe your son tried to take his casual attitude from high school into the university arena and found out professors aren't interested in excuses. All of a sudden, his degree — and four years of college tuition — is in jeopardy.

What do you do? These problems brought on by little or no discipline are serious, but they don't have to be life-threatening. Let's look at several areas that signal lack of discipline.

Putting Off 'Til Tomorrow

Procrastination is a cousin of poor discipline. They are closely-related.

If your loved one refuses to take care of daily things, you can be sure discipline has fallen by the wayside. No matter how much you point this out or threaten, an arrogance takes over the person, and he or she continues in this destructive pattern.

If the problem begins to draw in other people, watch out. If your teenager is buying a car from someone who has owner-financed the purchase, you might expect to see that owner on your doorstep one fine evening, wanting a few late payments. Now, someone else is affected by your son's irresponsible behavior.

The same can be said for the husband who has dis-creetly — or so he has thought — missed a few days of work.

Sitting in his recliner one evening, he can't get to the phone in time and his wife answers.

She repeats "uh-huh" a lot and finally slams the phone down. "That was your boss," she says angrily. "He wanted to know how seriously ill you were since you hadn't been to work all week."

Lack of discipline in one of the basic areas of life — work — brings with it a whole caldron of other problems.

The undisciplined person seems to have lost all sense of what is important in life. Often, he lives only for the moment and fails to see the far-reaching consequences of even small, seemingly insignificant lapses into irresponsibility.

Helping the Undisciplined

Do you see a pattern developing in the warning signs we listed? In each of them, the lack of discipline has progressed to the point that real problems are at hand. The family of the loved one in question didn't see the problems coming. *But what do you do?*

You won't have much luck if you rant and rave about the problem. If a shortage of discipline has brought a person to this level, how can they pull themselves up if you're yelling?

- Love them and encourage them.
- Help them set reasonable goals.
- Provide a mentor.
- Participate in their recovery.

The Bible teaches that God corrects His children in gentle ways, whenever possible. He pushes us along at a pace we can adjust to — unless a firm hand is needed. Here is one way in which God differs from us. He can become as adamant as He wants.

For us, we might get to a point where we realize our loved one is not going to change much. We may have to make a decision to accept them the way they are and love them anyway, or we can encourage them to change. When the fruit of the Spirit comes into a person's heart, he loves everybody. That means that you love people, even if you can't control them, or change them.

Setting Reasonable Goals

Since lack of discipline so often is akin to procrastination, help the loved one set reasonable goals. Most of us want to try and fix all our problems in one afternoon.

If the one we love responds favorably to your pointing out he or she is undisciplined, don't overwhelm by trying to deal with every area at the same time. Focus on the area that is having the most dramatic impact on their lives.

You might say, "Okay, today you need to concentrate on paying all your bills. Tomorrow you can talk to creditors." This will give the person the correct impression that progress is being made with the problem.

If the discipline problem has affected finances, depending on the severity of the problem, a trained financial counselor may be the answer. Once achieving a measure of success in discipline in one area, the challenge will be there to take on other areas that need work.

Procrastination sometimes has its roots in perfectionism and the fear of failure. A person will put off doing something that appears beyond his level of skill or expertise. It's like the student who waits until the night before his term paper is due to begin working on it.

To prevent last minute panic, sometimes all that's needed is for you to say, "Let's sit down together and figure out what you need to do first. This weekend you can take a few hours and go to the library and do your research. Next Saturday morning, you can write the rough draft, and the last weekend, you can type your paper."

Adults who are procrastinators can also benefit from someone helping them plan their activities. Sometimes, just talking over a project with another person or brain-storming with the family, can break that overwhelming sense of dread that we often feel when confronted by a task.

Getting Outside Help

If your loved one has difficulty accepting advice from you, find someone he will listen to — a mentor who can take them aside and work in their lives; a tutor for the poor math student; a weight-loss program for the overeater, etc.

Most people wouldn't think of getting professional help for a discipline problem, but show them the wisdom in this approach. Just concentrating on the discipline of meeting once a week with a mentor or professional therapist can illuminate other areas where your loved one needs help.

It was tough for me to acknowledge that I had a deep problem and that I needed to bring myself under discipline. When my esteemed friend, Dr. Arthur Parsons, offered to help me, I quickly realized this would be the opportunity of a lifetime to truly bring myself under the discipline of a righteous person who cared about my life. For four and a half years, we met each week for a consultation. He offered his loving concern and set the example.

Conclusion

We can just imagine what thoughts went through Joshua's mind as this successor to Moses was commanded by God to continue the work begun in Egypt. If Joshua had not developed discipline, he would have been tempted to bolt and run. Instead, this important character held fast and applied all the lessons Moses had taught him. He carried on the affairs of the Israelites with a firm hand. He led by example.

How important this is for us to remember when dealing with a problem involving discipline. It knows no age boundaries, no boundaries of any kind. If your own life is grounded in discipline, you will be less likely to have to deal with a loved one's problem in this area.

I am reminded of Samson, that powerful man of God who crumbled from lack of discipline. Allowing himself to be delivered to his enemies by a disloyal woman, how different it could have been had Samson maintained the discipline that made him feared far and wide.

Maintain your vigilance in the area of discipline and perhaps the roof won't cave in on you!

6

Failure

Plans fail for lack of counsel, but with many advisers they succeed.   Prov. 15:22

I know about failure and how I was helped when I stumbled. It is devastating. It is painful, it is ugly to be a public spectacle, to be laughed at, to be scorned. To hide from people and not want to show your face. I know that loss. And I have no one to blame but myself.

No problem is more personal than failure. No problem involves more shame. There are so many types of failures, it sometimes appears as if society is one great wasteland littered with the fallen.

Failure is one of Satan's greatest weapons. He has used it throughout the centuries to bring down kingdoms. It deeply hurts families and relationships. The pain of failure can split marriages and dissolve partnerships. And Satan wants us to stay where we are — and not get up. Satan laughs at failure. He feeds on it. It gives him a reason to go on.

Often at Life Challenge, our crisis agency, we counsel people who are immobilized because of some failure in their lives. It is heartbreaking to watch. Men who seemingly have no hope in restoring trust in their marriages; women who have succumbed to temptation in the workplace. Failure goes deeper than just losing a round of golf, losing an account for your firm, or being embarrassed by a public dismissal.

Failure is at the core of our being. Without God, we are doomed to fail — it is a part of our nature. Sometimes God permits it. Mankind is born into sin, or spiritual failure. God lets us do stupid, sinful things and if we humble ourselves and admit them, He can receive glory for himself and our miserable mistakes.

We have counseled literally hundreds of souls mired in a spirit of failure. Many, many people make the first step to finding restoration, but they cannot let go of the fact they have failed at something at some point in their lives. They cannot forgive themselves.

We don't want to dwell too much on lashing out at those who have failed spiritually. Do you know why? We'll tell you a little secret: *We have all sinned and come short of the glory of God.*

Every one of us.

Danger Signals

If you hope to help free someone you love from some failure, realize that without a compassionate spirit, you will be like a stalk of grass trying to block the path of a bulldozer. You will not be able to lift your hurting brother up out of the pit.

Determine that you will become immersed in living a victorious life. When your loved ones stumble along because of — or on the verge of — failure, ask yourself if they fit the following warning signs:

- They avoid those who know them best.
- They have a proud attitude.
- They have difficulty fending off temptation.
- They lie in order to retain their power.

If the failure is going to come as a surprise to you, it will come about because your loved one desired to hide it from you and the rest of the family. This person will literally ignore you or duck away when you show up. This will be very obvious with an outgoing person, but not so easily seen with an introvert. Still, any type of personality can fall into this warning sign. Their shame is too great.

When my world collapsed, God was so merciful to send three wonderful friends to help me, to love me, and to be there to hear my heart's cry. Rather than readily admitting my failures, I put on an Academy Award performance, implying that everything was all right — "We'll work our way through this" — and yet, in my heart, I knew I had failed and was too proud to admit my need of help. I really would rather have avoided people, because my shame was too immense.

Pride Before the Fall

Do you know why I failed personally? Because I missed out on the best God had for me. I didn't fail because I was incompetent or lazy, but I developed an attitude that said, "My abilities will see me through." This is very definitely the mark of a proud attitude.

I failed to heed the warning signs in my own life.

When a man called from the West Coast, telling me of his fraudulent activities, he was so afraid. He had embezzled over $5 million. When it all began, he really didn't need to do that to be a wealthy person, but pride so possessed him that he was willing to make any compromise necessary to retain his position of power. He wanted to be a mover and shaker, gain attention for himself, even in church circles.

But he was brought to an abrupt halt when his crimes were discovered.

From God's perspective, he didn't spend time in prison for fraud alone, but it was his proud heart that brought about his downfall.

Can't Stop the Failure

Another way to tell if your loved one is being damaged by failure is if he or she *fails to stop the failure*. This might happen the day after the two of you have had a heart-to-heart talk, and the loved one has pledged all sorts of things: "I am going to start doing better today." "I'll turn over a new leaf." This usually occurs when the failure involves some character flaw, like infidelity or stealing. They can't resist temptation. There is a pattern.

Susan was a professional person and the day she walked into my office, I was impressed as she talked to me about her many talents. Her future seemed so bright. She had been ordered by the police to come see me because she had been repeatedly caught shoplifting. She had a responsible position in the community and church, and she was loved. But it gave me insight I didn't have before when she said, "It's not things I need, but when I see some object in a store, it's almost like a sexual experience. I feel I must have the object. At the risk of my own character, I take it." She looked down before continuing, "I don't need it, but at that moment, I feel like I have to grab it. I will never do it again."

Several times we had that visit. It did not stop until she was arrested and suffered a severe consequence.

Lying to Retain Power

For many people, lying to retain power surges ahead until it's out of control. The thirst for a better position, more influence, and greater latitude results in an obvious display. Your loved one will tell lies that *you* will recognize, even if no one else does. Some people are willing to let things slide and let the truth be butchered in order to keep the peace.

We will always be out of control until we learn to truly discipline ourselves and be accountable to God and others.

Doing Your Part

Since we have all failed at some point in our lives, helping someone else through the crisis of failure is not as difficult as some of the other issues we have dealt with in this book. Here are a few suggestions:

- Discourage self-examination and condemnation.
- Be available.
- Encourage them to come clean.
- Share your own failures with them.

Some people teach that men and women suffer through failure because of something they have done wrong in their personal lives. If that were the case, we would all fail regularly. Many failures in life result from circumstances beyond your control.

In the third chapter of Daniel, three young fellows named Shadrack, Meshack, and Abednego defied King Nebuchadnezzar, who had sent a decree that everyone was to fall down and worship his image. These three young men politely declined, saying they would worship only the God of Israel. For this slap at the king, they were thrown into a fiery furnace. When they emerged from the flames without even a trace of smoke on their clothing, it was a miraculous day indeed!

Where was the failure in the lives of these three men that brought on a burning punishment? Bad things happen to good people, as the book title goes. The Bible is full of stories like this.

You can help a loved one recognize that just because they are enduring some persecution at the moment, they need not examine their own lives to find some huge, hidden sin. In many cases, it just simply isn't there. And yet, these tortured souls search and search for the elusive sin that has caused a valley experience. If there is something wrong on a "personal level," God knows our hearts.

When Howard sat in my office with his wife's loving embrace comforting him, I knew he was walking through a deep valley.

"Pastor Dortch," he slowly began, "I've been told I will not live for more than four or five months. I am searching my heart and preparing for eternity." In many years of working with wonderful people all over the world, I had never met a more kind, loving, Christ-like person. After he had been smitten with cancer, out of a pure heart he had sincerely sought the Lord. Some mean-spirited "false prophets" had come to Howard and his wife and said, "If only you would get sin out of your lives, you'd be healed." As I watched them, I knew it had been almost as painful as the news about the cancer. It was a wicked blow from people not in a position to have a kind word about anything. I assured Howard and his wife that God loved them and would take care of them, and was certainly holding nothing against them.

Get Involved

If, on the other hand, you can tell that a loved one has brought about a problem through self-destructive behavior, you can gently point this out and offer solutions. One solution is to help them monitor their destructive patterns. Help them stay out of compromising situations.

Explain to them what temptation is and how it waits like a viper under a rock. This can entail suggesting they enter a different line of work or stop associating with people who tempt them.

It isn't enough to just say, "You need to watch that."

You must be willing to say, "Look, instead of hanging

out with that crowd, come with me, and we'll do something constructive."

Be available!

If an individual wants to hide from the world following some failure, point out to them that the longer they maintain a very low profile, the longer the situation will stick in people's minds. Making full disclosure is so important. Just ask a few ex-presidents of this great country.

It is said that Americans love to forgive a politician and get on with things. That should be the active motto of Christians. Forgive failure — since we all have it, anyway — and move on. Love them out of their self-imposed exile.

Helping a loved one overcome failure should not be a mystery to us. We all have experience with it. Your own story of how you got past failure is sure to encourage that hurting brother, grandparent, cousin, or friend.

Conclusion

God wants a victorious life for each of us. Unfortunately, since Satan uses the tactic of failure incessantly, millions of people are unable to be an effective witness for Christ. Failure was not intended for humanity, but if it is here, then we must fight it.

But not alone.

When we bring ourselves under God's design and submit ourselves to others, we can be sure that the test we are walking through "will surely pass." The sun will rise tomorrow and you will see more clearly what you have learned, and how you can help others.

7

Forgiveness

*Bear with each other and forgive whatever
grievances you may have against one another.
Forgive as the Lord forgave you.* Col. 4:8

I am fortunate to have friends, true friends. When my
world collapsed and I wondered if I would ever have a future
again, my beloved friend, Jamie Buckingham, cared enough
about me to not let me go.

When a literary agent and the publishers in New York
City called about me writing a book detailing what happened in the national scandal I was involved in, Jamie
accompanied me to New York.

"If you will write a book about working for Jerry
Falwell, we will sign on for your book," one publisher said.
The bidding began in the six-figure range. It's obvious what
$100,000 or more could have meant. Jamie constantly
reminded me the story was not over — there was more to
come.

Whatever disagreements I may have had with Jerry Falwell, I knew I could not engage in writing a book whose purpose was to deliberately hurt someone. I couldn't do it. It meant more to me to have a tender, forgiving heart than to have any amount of money.

I need a forgiving spirit every day of my life. I don't really know of anything that helps me more in family situations, in business, the church, in my work, and personal relationships. I have learned that looking in the rear-view mirror will only get you into big trouble!

Forgiveness is the Great Ignored Principle in today's Church. And yet, Jesus emphasized the concept repeatedly. He commanded us to forgive. It isn't an option.

Jesus said, "If you forgive men their trespasses, your heavenly Father will forgive you your trespasses."

Sadly, forgiveness is approached in two different ways by a majority today, especially so-called Christians.

One way is to say, "I'll forgive, but I won't forget it!"

The other responds, "I can't forgive — the pain is too great."

God forgave all of our evil sins — sending His only Son to die on the cross. Sometimes we seek justification for the wrongs we've endured. But that is not the way that brings the best results. We're too good. We've been wronged just a little too much.

God have mercy on us.

Forgiveness is more than a word. It is running out and doing something about it. It is embracing the one who needs forgiving.

For centuries, scoffers have ridiculed the advice of Jesus, who said, "Love your enemies," as being impractical, idealistic, and absurd. Satan tells us that to forgive is to be weak. Nobody wants to be thought of as a weakling. Besides, revenge feels good, right? This is a practice actively encouraged in many churches.

Ironically, psychiatrists and physicians are recommending it as one of the greatest antidotes of man's ills.

Jesus said we are to forgive "seventy times seven." That means we aren't to forgive just 490 times, but indefinitely, forever.

This is one way we cure those ulcers and other diseases ravaging our bodies. Did you ever think about it that way? Did you ever suppose that the cause of your bodily ailments is an unforgiving spirit?

Making a Diagnosis

Spotting the warning signs for one who has a problem with forgiveness is one of the easiest diagnoses we can make. Those who are harboring unforgiveness have certain characteristics:

- They develop a bitter spirit.
- Inexplicable illnesses attack their body and mind.
- Scores of damaged relationships trail behind them.
- They are highly critical of others.

How many bitter people do you know? It is a sad state of affairs when we know more mean people than we do nice ones. It's as if a whole host of demons has descended on this once-peaceful life of ours and whispered the words, "Don't forgive," to every man, woman, and child.

Until the ministry and spirit of forgiveness penetrates our spirits, the depths of love and forgiveness such as expressed in Jesus *cannot be understood!* You become a slave to those you will not forgive. The moment you start hating a person, you become hounded by him. You cannot escape his tyrannical grasp on your mind; he controls your thoughts.

Do we really want to be that way?

Dr. S.I. McMillen, in his eye-opening book, *None of*

These Diseases, outlines in fascinating detail the cost on the body of harboring bitterness:

> Running down people does not keep us free from a host of diseases of body and mind. The verbal expression of animosity toward others calls forth certain hormones from the pituitary, adrenal, thyroid, and other glands, an excess of which can cause disease in any part of the body.[1]

I have come across many people crippled by physical pain and disease, who all the while are cursing their fellow man and woman. This is no mystery, dear reader. An unforgiving spirit kills in more ways than one.

Try to name elderly people who are bitter you've come across in your life. They seldom go together. Hatred and old age don't mix. It is a perspective we need to address.

On the other hand, it would take me a solid week to recount for you all the times I've seen miraculous, instantaneous healing take place when forgiveness is allowed to bloom.

When Ted finally understood he was taken advantage of by another Christian, he was enraged. He would not let go. When he came into my life, his wife told me, "It's killing him." When she called early one morning and gave me the fearful news of his death, I tried to probe as to why — was it a heart attack? What was it? Through her tears, his wife said, "His doctors say it was his heart. I believe it was probably his anger." He would not forgive.

Who Is the Real Problem?

Another obvious sign of an unforgiving spirit is the littered trail of damaged friendships. A person who is bitter has often been that way for years, and their track record in broken relationships is a long one. When you see someone who can't get along with *anyone*, you can rest assured the people they do battle with aren't the problem.

I once knew a college girl who couldn't settle on a roommate. She went through them like water. Each one caused her to moan pitifully that they did this or they did that to her. In reality, she chased them all away.

It isn't a mystery why relationships are destroyed, and we shouldn't pretend it is.

Blasting the Barnacles

Helping someone in this situation is one of the most difficult things any of us will face. Bitterness attaches itself like barnacles on a ship. Blasting powder might be needed to remove it. Here are some suggestions that may help.

- Confront them with their bitterness.
- Tell them that forgiveness is a choice.
- Show them how to forgive themselves.

For those harboring a bitter spirit, point out to them that they don't have to respond to everything that happens; sometimes the best answer is no answer. They really can walk away. If they are engaged in a struggle with someone over, say, a land deal gone sour, it is in their best interests to leave the other person alone.

Are you afraid to confront the one with a bitter spirit? God has spelled out clearly for us that those who refuse to forgive will not enter His eternal kingdom. Recorded in Matthew 18 is the story of the unmerciful servant who owed his king 10,000 talents. The debtor begged for a little more time to pay the bill, and the king granted amnesty.

Soon afterward, the same servant accosted one of his own debtors and immediately asked him to pay the hundred pence he owed (a pittance compared to the 10,000 talents). The second servant asked for more time but was flatly refused.

The king, being told by others who were outraged at what was done, called the wicked servant back in and said these terse words:

> . . . I forgave thee all that debt, because thou desiredst me:
> Shouldest not thou also have had compassion on they fellowservant, even as I had pity on thee?
> And his lord was wroth, and delivered him to the tormentors, till he should pay all that was due unto him.
> So likewise shall my heavenly Father do also unto you, if ye from your hearts forgive not every one his brother their trespasses (Matt. 18:32-35).

People live in torment because they will not forgive. Without going into details that would embarrass the person involved, let me give a quick example.

I was preaching in a church, and after the service a woman came up to me.

"Pastor Dortch," the lady said, "I have harbored something against you for 28 years, and I want to ask your forgiveness."

Needless to say, I was shocked! I had no idea what she was talking about.

"You probably don't even remember me," she continued, "but when you were just out of Bible college, you used to date my close friend. You had even planned to marry."

It was true. Before Mildred and I knew God had given us to each other, I had been engaged to someone else. Several things happened to help me see that I should marry Mildred, so I had broken off the first relationship. Everything had ended amicably between the other girl, her family, and me.

"I was supposed to be in the wedding party," the woman interrupted my thoughts, "and when you broke off the engagement, I was very hurt for my friend and disappointed about the wedding plans. All these years, I have kept that bitterness locked inside. I've watched you on television and seen your picture in magazines. Each time was a reminder of how hurt I had been."

She once again asked my forgiveness, and I asked hers, but I felt so sad for her as I walked away from that conversation. How tragic that she had carried unforgiveness against me for a quarter-century, and the person she refused to forgive wasn't even aware of her hurt!

Churches, unfortunately, are filled with unforgiving people. We carry grudges against others. We build walls instead of bridges.

I've met people who become so "anti-faith movement" that they wish Kenneth Hagin would get seriously ill so he could be proven wrong! I've seen others who secretly gloat when any of the prosperity-oriented ministries have financial problems.

Can God bless such rabid examples of bitterness and unforgiveness? I cannot believe that the Father enjoys seeing us put each other in walled compartments.

"He who cannot forgive others," George Herbert once wrote, "breaks the bridge over which he must pass himself." Remember, we must be willing to get down in the slop with the hogs if we truly want to help them.

Confront that person with their sin! You don't have to yell and scream. In fact, you'll be amazed at the progress you'll make by repeating the command of God to forgive.

You can help a person who has a problem with unforgiveness by making them aware of that trail of broken relationships. Quietly show them that many of these situations could have been avoided. Again, be prepared for an onslaught of hearing how disloyal you are, etc. But if the person is smart, the talk will sink in.

This solution to an unforgiving spirit is not for the faint-of-heart. It will be difficult. But dissolving years of strife and pain in a hardened heart will be the greatest miracle your eyes have seen.

I remember a lady in our church who spent decades in physical pain. Wheelchair-bound and wracked with incredible sufferings, she did not take it like a saint. In fact, she often listed all those who had "done her wrong" in life.

Finally, almost out of desperation, I knelt down one morning after services and asked her, "Would you like to be relieved of your pain?"

She looked at me with surprise and nodded excitedly. I knew she expected me to lay hands on her and bathe us both in a supernatural light right there in the sanctuary.

Instead, I told her softly, "My dear, you must forgive your enemies." At those words, she contorted her face and spat insults at me. It was horrifying.

But there is a happy ending. Weeks later, she entered the church house . . . walking! She had discarded her wheelchair when she abandoned her hatred for her fellow man. What a blessing she was to our congregation.

Physical ailments don't just come out of the air. Ask your loved one to stop the hatred and stand back to watch the results. They might lash out at you initially, but later, in their quiet times, come back to the Lord. Impress upon them the importance of "swallowing the medicine" and forgiving and asking for forgiveness.

Choosing to Forgive

Before you can help someone else, you may need to deal with the unforgiveness in your own heart. You may even have resentment against the very person you are trying to help!

God uses some people to irritate us. How easy it is for us to magnify the peculiarities of others and to harp on the ways certain folks aggravate us. God sometimes shows us how we as individuals need to practice forgiveness in order to receive it.

At other times, our anger smolders at wrongs someone has done to us. Sometimes, these wrongs are the products of our own imagination. Here again, we become *bound*, instead of *free*. Your loved one must become aware of this and see it for the killer it is.

We cannot know the blessing of God if we are holding onto our sins.

When we choose not to forgive a wrong, we do so because we want to hurt, *really hurt,* the person in question. And do you know what that gets us? We become slaves to the very people we don't forgive! Yes, we become captives to them because we allow their memory to control us and poison us. Yet, they may not even be aware of it.

We are not free when we choose not to forgive.

Not one of us is free of guilt when it comes to unforgiveness. There is no need to point the finger of accusation at others unless we search our own hearts and recognize and confess this great sin ourselves.

I am human. I get critical, and I have prayed about it. But my problem is not with someone else — it's with me!

I must constantly practice the concept of forgiveness because who am I to cherish resentment when God has forgiven me for so much? Jesus tells us first to be reconciled to our brother, then to come to Him in worship. This is not easy for it requires the grace of humility. But what peace and joy it brings to the one who is so reconciled.

Some of us will miss out on the great joy that comes from being in God's will because we do not forgive.

Forgiving Yourself

Don't think all unforgiveness is aimed at other people.

Have you ever failed to forgive yourself? Self-forgiveness is so prevalent and, at the same time, so suppressed.

As a result, we become depressed. Sometimes it takes a while before we realize that our depression stems from not forgiving ourselves.

This explains why a person who has painstakingly gone through each relationship in his or her life and steadfastly forgiven wrongs still has feelings of restlessness and searching. That person hasn't practiced self-forgiveness!

Just as our Father is pleased when we forgive others, so, too, is He delighted when we unshackle ourselves from the guilt we carry around.

As you seek to help the one you love overcome their unforgiveness, you may want to look within your own heart and see if some hidden resentment is buried there. If so, do as we have suggested. Confront it. Identify the person who is the focus of your unforgiveness, and then choose to forgive. Go one step further and forgive yourself for harboring an unforgiving spirit against that person. Now praise the Lord for His mercy and forgiveness toward you.

Now you are ready to let go and let God use you to help those you love.

Conclusion

Have you noticed the factions existing in some denominations today? At the root of the division is a spirit of unforgiveness. It doesn't matter what caused that attitude — it's here, now.

People inside and outside of churches embrace all sorts of causes. They have special committees and clusters of members here and there, all keeping tabs on each other. If they could only see that if they don't embrace forgiveness, and let it heal their hearts and minds, the "noble causes" will be worthless.

What lost person will listen to us if we carry a Bible in one hand, and a hammer for bashing our brethren in the other?

Forgive. Why? Because Jesus wants us to be free.

Notes

[1] S.I. McMillan, *None of These Diseases* (Grand Rapids, MI: Baker Book House/Revell, 1985).

8

Admitting Mistakes

Humble yourselves, therefore, under God's mighty hand, that he may lift you up in due time.
1 Pet. 5:6

I know about admitting mistakes. When I came out of my failure, I made it a point to ask forgiveness from every congregation I spoke to. In fact, I still do this.

I went to Dallas one year to attend the Christian Booksellers Association convention, and while there I spoke at a large church. As we neared the church, I wondered, *Would there be the crowd they were expecting?* Perhaps only the local congregation would know I was coming. But as we came to the freeway exit for the church, a giant marquee loomed ahead of us, announcing Richard Dortch as that morning's guest speaker. Most of the convention attendees would surely have seen the sign on their way in from the airport. There was no hope of escape now.

Immediately I knew what I had to do. I was "made to

know" — this is the way I describe God's promptings to me — that I must confess my sins and ask forgiveness, apologizing to the people of the church that morning for the hurt and reproach I had brought on the gospel. I knew that was the right thing to do, and with God's grace I could do it.

The members and pastor lovingly greeted Mildred and me as we made our way into the church. After a few choruses and the opening prayer, I stood to my feet and, with trembling knees and breaking heart, approached the pulpit.

"Pastor," I began, my voice barely above a whisper, "thank you for your kind introduction, but please stay here at the pulpit with me. There is some unfinished business I need to do before I speak."

Silence filled the cathedral. I could sense the audience waiting for my next word.

"This church," I continued, "has been a friend to Mildred and me for many years. I hurt you, Pastor. I brought shame to my friends, this church, and the body of Christ. I brought reproach to you as a person and to this group of people, and for this I am very sorry. I ask each of you to forgive me, and I plead with this congregation to forgive me. I know God has forgiven me, but now I need to ask you to forgive me because I so regret the pain I brought into your lives."

As I ceased talking, I felt as if time itself had stopped. The audience appeared stunned by my confession. All the respected people I had expected to be there were seated throughout the church that morning. Yet, through God's grace, I faced my sins and publicly confessed the things I had done wrong.

I waited for what seemed like eternity, then I heard a sob, and then another. Someone stood and began to weep. Then I felt the warm arm of Pastor George around me. With tears, he hugged me intensely, whispering, "You are forgiven." At that moment I was lost in a world of love.

When I regained my composure, the congregation was standing, some applauding, some weeping. I looked at them through my tears, wondering what had just happened and what would happen next.

After a few minutes, the people quieted down, and Pastor George stepped to the microphone. "Richard Dortch," he said, looking directly into my eyes, "you are forgiven. We want you to know the peace we have all found. Never again to this congregation need you say anything about the past. We forgive you, just as we have been forgiven. You are loved."

The majesty of the moment was overwhelming. Not the majesty of my being center stage, or in front of many of the mighty men and women of faith I knew and respected. The majesty of that moment came from within. It came as I asked forgiveness for my sins.

After my confession before the believers of Calvary Church, I determined that if I must go before every congregation that invites me to speak and confess my failure, I would do it.

Although confessing my sin and asking and receiving forgiveness brought great healing to my heart and mind, I knew the process was not complete. I needed to do more than confess to others; I needed to confront myself. I knew I had to search my soul to discover the reasons for my transgressions and downfall.

After many months of self-examination and near total despair, I identified the root of my sin: I had violated the power entrusted to me by God and by my brothers and sisters in the faith. I had tried to seize some of God's glory, and He would have none of it.

I feel it is important to stand up and face our mistakes, and I continually strive to monitor my progress in this area. Some of our mistakes come from greed. It can affect all of us. Now I stay away from the things I don't need and instead, concentrate on the things that will help me and people I care about.

Adults who will stand up and admit their mistakes are

extremely hard to find in today's society. There is hardly a more pervasive problem anywhere. No one wants to take the blame or admit they have blown it.

How about you? Do you admit your mistakes? Are you willing to be free to ask the one you love to do the same?

Let's get rid of the word "can't." We *can* admit mistakes — but some of us *won't*. That is part of our nature. No one wants to look bad or lose face.

The one you love may have this problem. If so, it is possible they also have a problem with lying. He or she can't admit when they're wrong, so they lie to themselves while they try to hide the truth from others.

Let's consider two men as we explore this problem of failure to admit mistakes.

The first man is a composite of some of our best-selling books. His entire focus in life is the big ME. Some of our most popular books have given us envy-producing, narcissistic slogans:

"Looking out for Number One!"

"Winning through intimidation!"

"You *can* have it all!"

This kind of thinking has produced an incredible attitude of arrogance in our society. As we get away from God, we decide that our law is final. We won't admit a mistake — even an obvious one.

I received a compelling letter from a man who had read my book, *Fatal Conceit*. He had embezzled over $100,000 and when he read the book, it shook him and helped him to realize he must admit his crime. When he called, he not only confirmed what the letter said, but told me that his mind had so blocked his sin that he thought he was getting away with it. I shared with him a little trade secret I've learned: God already knows about our sin.

Keep in mind this attitude started with the most beautiful angel ever created. Not content with the joyful work of remaining in the presence of the Lord, Lucifer, at some terrible point, crossed the line of arrogance. Imagine him in counsel with the renegade angels who followed after him. He looked at them and would not admit that he had made a mistake in his rebellion.

The rest is history gone wrong.

Satan is the ultimate example of pride that refuses to take the blame.

The other man I want to consider is remembered as one of the great prophets of God.

So far as we know, Isaiah was a young man of excellent character. He had the respect and confidence of all who knew him. But when he got a glimpse of God's infinite holiness, he cried out, "Woe is me, for I am undone, because I am of unclean lips, and I dwell in the midst of a people of unclean lips; for mine eyes have seen the king, the Lord of hosts" (Isa. 6:5).

Isaiah saw himself as he was. He knew himself better than his associates knew him.

Which person are you? Are you humble, or prideful? God hates self-righteousness simply because He knows what we are really like. Our pride disgusts Him.

Common Characteristics

Two friends were talking about a husband and wife they knew — a couple who couldn't get along.

"Who will win?" one asks.

"The one who quits arguing or attacking!" the other answers.

How true. But few of us are humble enough to give up our rights and our opinions and let the other person have the last say.

Is your loved one the one who refuses to quit arguing or attacking? How do you identify a problem, if it exists? Those who refuse to admit their mistakes have certain common characteristics in their behavior:

- They are involved in frequent arguments.
- They lack genuine humility.
- Their complaints don't ring true.
- They will never admit to any failure.

In dissecting the first warning sign, think about how often arguments occur. One per week is too much.

These situations escalate, starting out few in number and before you know it, several arguments a week are the norm. And by "argument," I'm talking about a heated exchange.

The person who refuses to admit mistakes will never want to agree with you. This will increase the frequency and volume of arguments, and you risk harming yourself by being pulled into these types of confrontations.

Remember when Pharaoh and Moses clashed repeatedly as God prepared to set His people free? Time after time, Moses approached the king of Egypt with the command from God to give the Israelites their freedom. Each time, Pharaoh refused. He wouldn't admit he was wrong.

As a result, several terrible events plagued him and his people, not the least of which was death itself. Pharaoh was one of the most visible examples in history of someone who wouldn't admit his mistakes. His pride brought ruin to his nation and to his house.

Tricky Propositions

The next warning sign is a little more subtle. Detecting a lack of true humility in a person can be a tricky proposition. There are so many variables to consider.

The one you love might find delight in pointing out the mistakes of others, all the while, *their faults* are very apparent to everyone but themselves. This likely won't be a passing problem, or a new one. This type of personality is developed over years. We know that God can change that, but He needs our participation.

The more possible scenario is that you will have to help the person work through the problem.

Another warning sign is one we can all relate to. We get tired of hearing one excuse after another.

Shakespeare once wrote about it, and I paraphrase: "I think you protest too much." It doesn't take long to figure out that your loved one's excuses don't relate to the facts.

Your daughter comes home with a note from the teacher explaining that she has been caught cheating on a test. At first, you side with your daughter, but the next week, another note. And another. Finally, you have to confront your child and demand the truth.

Parents who defend their children in their mistakes are not helping the child. Encouraging the child to admit their behavior can be redemptive.

You might find this example quaint and really non-threatening, but fast-forward a few years. Susie is accused of having an affair with a married man. Then another accusation. Another. Ferreting out someone who refuses to tell the truth in this situation is not difficult.

Getting Off the Merry-Go-Round

Now, how do you go about helping a person in this situation? Old habits of lying and covering mistakes die hard.

- Break the argument cycle.
- Discuss the importance of humility.
- Confront them with their lies.
- Show them the value of telling the truth.

Depending on your personality, you can try explaining to the person that you're getting off the merry-go-round of arguing since nothing positive is accomplished. Escalating arguments can become abusive — emotionally so, if nothing else. Remember that the cycle of constant arguing does *nothing* to help the one you love. It plays into their hands. Nothing good comes of it. It aggravates the situation.

If you're dealing with someone who doesn't have an attitude of humility, consider that unless they develop it on their own, life will do it for them. Point out that embarrassing mistakes are bound to occur unless an attitude change comes about.

To help someone who won't admit mistakes and lies to cover them, take an active role instead of a passive one. Lovingly confront and point out that, at the very least, the story sounds phony. Very few people will call someone an out-and-out liar, especially a loved one, but the non-admission of mistakes will only deepen as time goes on.

It is my experience in my life and ministry, and in encountering people who have had failures, that many would rather lie than admit a mistake. I have been involved in thousands of cases with ministers and laymen and in almost all these situations we've confronted, people have not told the truth.

Sadly, my experience has also been that Christians generally are not any more forthcoming than unbelievers. Our pride is much deeper than our love of the truth.

This solution is in keeping with our quest of deciding whether we really want to help someone we love. How far are you willing to go in this walk the loved one is taking?

Conclusion

Admitting mistakes is one of the most distasteful things any of us will ever have to do. It goes against our nature. Humility, a conciliatory attitude — these things require us to expose our weaknesses to others. But it is a central part of being a Christian.

If you don't believe in old-time miracles, or if you have never seen one, just watch a brother or sister who gets right with friends and family hurt by mistakes that were never acknowledged. Years of strife will melt away and become harmless memories if we humble ourselves and admit our mistakes.

Living in shame is a miserable thing. Admitting our mistakes sets us free.

Our Heavenly Father already knows about mistakes. We can be free when we admit them.

9

Sharing Love

Do not seek revenge or bear a grudge against one of your people, but love your neighbor as yourself. I am the Lord.   Lev. 9:18

Love is available to all of us, but too many consider it to be a mystery, and, therefore, they are uncomfortable sharing their love. Husbands don't share with wives; parents withhold love from their children; sisters and brothers harbor grudges for years. It's tragic.

I am reminded of the man who was revered as a Christian counselor in his hometown. He worked painstakingly over each case, ministering to the hurting, offering encouragement, and sharing in the healing his office brought to his friends and associates.

And yet, when this smiling, gregarious man walked through the front door of his home every night, his family was greeted by a dour, silent figure who spent hours alone in his study, brooding. This great counselor couldn't show love to his own family.

The kingdom of God is hindered because so many of us so-called Christians show so little evidence of Christian love! The healing balm of love is desperately needed in a world where Satan tempts us to do the very opposite.

But I have good news!

As I emerged from my valley experiences in the last few years, I was dumbfounded by the outpouring of love shown me by friends, family, and even strangers. I saw love being shared in action, so I know it can be done. I know it is attainable for the masses.

The apostle Paul tells us that God will teach us to love others, even the most unlovely. "Through love be servants of one another. For the whole law is fulfilled in one word, 'You shall love your neighbor as yourself' " (Matt. 19:19).

Why is this so difficult for us to do? Why do we have an epidemic of love-starved wives in America? Why are so many husbands so lonely? There are millions of households in which family members can't or won't share their love with the people who need it most. Someone needs to be the aggressor in the environment in which love can be explored. You can be that person.

Some of the Reasons

Have you ever noticed how the one you love can be outgoing, even perky, to total strangers — and then greet you with an icy stare and silence? This is so prevalent.

There are almost unlimited reasons as to why people have a problem sharing love — the love that is from Christ. Here are a few warning signs from a person with this problem:

- They are friendly to acquaintances, but silent with family.
- They refuse to take part in family activities.
- They decline all social invitations.

• They seldom reach out to other people.

We've discussed the spouse who opens up to those outside the home but who remains cool within. Let's take that a bit deeper and analyze loved ones who close themselves off from family gatherings or activities.

Suppose your husband finds insignificant reasons to avoid your family. It has nothing to do with his job because the outing you've planned takes place on a Saturday. He knows weeks in advance about it, but when the weekend comes, he suddenly has to clean out the garage.

Now, you can tell yourself that it's really an isolated incident. But it will probably happen again and again. You can cover for a while, but then this aloofness becomes embarrassing and open.

Does the man who cannot accept and love his wife's family love his wife? One needs to find the reasons for our neglect and resistance to the one we should love. Open the subject, talk about it.

Let us consider a young single woman who declines social invitations. Perhaps these are offers from nice men to go somewhere together or friends who want to play "cupid." Of course, a young lady has every right to pick and choose her own dates, but suppose she keeps up this behavior for years. Pretty soon, she is at an age where all her friends are married and having children or even grandchildren.

If there is not an outward problem, what is the reason she can't accept and show love? Perhaps she has unrealistic expectations. There is love for everyone who seeks it.

Self-Contained Love

Years ago, a single lady school teacher finally married at the age of 35. When they learned she was unable to bear children, her husband, a kind and gentle man, suggested they adopt.

Although they did not actively pursue adoption, someone came to them and said, "I know two children who have been recently orphaned — a boy of three and a girl of five. Would you be interested in adopting them as your own?"

The husband rejoiced at this opportunity, but the wife began to consider all the problems that might come from taking "strangers" into their home. An immaculate housekeeper, she wondered how much their lives would have to change to accommodate these two young children.

After much consideration, she told her husband, "I cannot do it. I don't think I can love someone else's children. Besides, how can I continue to teach school and raise two youngsters?"

The husband tried to reason with her, saying, "We can work it out. I'm sure we can grow to love them like our own." But no amount of talking could convince the wife otherwise, and the social worker eventually found another couple to adopt the children.

Today, this woman is 85 years old and widowed. Although she is still quite active and even continues to drive her own car, she constantly struggles with loneliness and depression. Her husband left her well-off financially, and she has friends and relatives who care for her, but she now realizes that children are indeed "an inheritance from the Lord."

Her inability to share her love with "one of the least of these" built a wall of self-centeredness and bitterness around this woman that alienates many who know her. I can't help but wonder, if she had opened her heart to those orphaned children, that instead of feeling alone in her last years she could be surrounded by loving grandchildren.

You know someone like this, don't you? We all do. Although it is too late for this elderly woman, you may be able to help someone else avoid the heartache that withholding our love can bring.

How do we help them overcome these problems?

Where Does Love Come From?

We should strive every day to be loving as our Lord is loving. We can't expect to know His sweet spirit unless we are willing to demonstrate it in our lives toward the people who mean something to us.

What are some ways we can bridge the gap that separates us from those who can't share love?

- Lead them to the Lord of love.
- Instruct them by your living example of loving.
- Teach them about the fruit of the Spirit.

Before we can expect anyone to share their love, they must feel loved themselves. Most people, however, are searching for love in all the wrong places. You need to point them toward the One who doesn't just offer love but who is love. The apostle John said, "God is love."

In order to experience God's love, your loved one must first acknowledge their sin and their need for a Savior. Using your Bible or a good gospel tract, you can take them through the salvation Scriptures and offer to pray a prayer of confession and acceptance of Jesus Christ with them.

If you feel unprepared to do this, ask someone who is experienced at soul-winning to accompany you. Or, suggest your loved one attend a loving church where the gospel is preached and lived. When I went through the most difficult time of my life, it was a loving church, Pinellas Park Wesleyan Church, that came seeking me to worship with them. Never once did anyone bring up my past failures or sins. Larry and Pat Freeman, the pastors, and the wonderful congregation, also loved us. Seek out and find that type of church. Be sure you go to church together and learn about loving.

Once they have received Christ into their hearts, they have made the first step toward living a life of love. There are many excellent books that can help you, or you may want to seek out a pastor who can minister to the one you love.

Without the power of the Holy Spirit, the ability to share love will remain a difficult goal. The indwelling Spirit can empower us to live a Spirit-filled life.

As Christians walking with God, we need to be reminded that the real purpose of loving is to give of ourselves, not to have power. The real purpose of being filled with the Spirit is *that we might develop a Christ-like character.*

The Christian life is "Christ in you," flowing out of the nature and character of God himself! To have the fruit of the Spirit is to have love in your heart and mind for your fellow man. You can't be exclusive with this love.

And it is sometimes hard to love certain people (this may not even be their fault).

A man came to our counseling center and told us he only had one month to live. We didn't expect him to go around shouting, "Hallelujah!" But neither could we refuse to share our love with him. He had a need. We helped him to find a place among people who'd love him. People called him, wrote him, loved him.

Conclusion

We are to enter into one another's sorrows and bear one another's burdens and so fulfill the law of Christ. It isn't a smorgasbord deal, where we can take this but not that. We must embrace this concept of sharing love because it is from Christ himself.

For Mildred and me, we were fortunate to have had families who loved us, who set an example before us and helped us understand Jesus better by loving one another. It was an esteemed friend and his dear wife who showed such magnanimous love to us, that helped get us back on our feet. Arthur and Usteena Parsons were, for us, the most loving people the way they stood by our side, and still do to this day. They have become an extension of God's love to Mildred and me.

10

Sharing Dreams

*Command them to do good, to be rich in good
deeds, and to be generous and willing to share.*
1 Tim. 6:6

You aren't a loser, are you? Of course not. No one wants
to be a loser. Especially in our society.

Athletic teams spend millions of dollars each year to get
to the championship game. It is not the American way to be
a loser.

But let me tell you, if you close yourself off from those
around you, the ones you love, you are a loser. You lose
those chances for loving and for sharing dreams. Being
alone is a set-up for losing.

Men sometimes have a problem relating to their own
families. This seems to be a male trait, but it is not limited
to the male sex. Women also are sometimes reluctant to
open up to those who love them, holding back on sharing
their most intimate dreams.

What of this concept of not sharing your dreams? We share other things — food, conversation, ideas. We might even share intimately with those we love but are shy about sharing the dreams of our hearts.

I have never had a problem sharing my visions or goals with Mildred. We make decisions together, and after all these years of marriage, she practically knows what I'm thinking, anyway. But, I do not take that for granted. We still enjoy listening to one another's hopes and dreams.

Dr. Martin Luther King shared his dream of society with us all one day many years ago. The television images of his stirring "I Have a Dream" speech still inspire me. Dr. King brought the best out in all of us when he shared his vision of what it would be like to live in a world where Jesus' teachings could become reality.

Martin Luther King wasn't afraid to share that giant dream, and his courage is with us today.

When Dreams are Shared

I knew since childhood that someday I would be involved in radio and television. It was my dream to share Christ's love with people all over the world. It was a dream of mine to start radio stations in my home state. That dream kept me alive for many years, and God was kind to let me see that dream come to pass. We were able to start three radio stations.

Let your dreams be a compelling force in your life.

There is an exhilaration that comes from sharing dreams — a thrill for yourself and the one you love. Many people, however, don't know what that joy is like. It goes back to closing yourself off from people.

Why does this happen? Some people may have a suspicious nature, having never learned to trust others. This may be the result of an abusive father or the heartache left from divorce. Or maybe they have tried to share their dreams only to be told their ideas are stupid or not possible.

This often happens to children or young people who are discovering new experiences in life.

One day your son sees the movie, *Raiders of the Lost Ark,* and rushes to tell you he wants to become an archeologist.

What do you say? "Do you know how much education it takes to be an archeologist? It's not the adventuresome lifestyle you see in the movies! It's mostly digging around in hard soil in the hot sun in some desert. Is that what you want for your life? Besides, you'll never make any money being an archeologist. And don't expect us to support you for the rest of your life!"

The dream is dashed, crushed in a million pieces on the kitchen floor and trampled by an insensitive adult who failed to recognize the exhilaration of having a dream.

What could have been said? "That's interesting, son. You've always liked history, and I can see where you would find archeology exciting. Maybe we can get you a subscription to *National Geographic* or *Biblical Archeology,* then you can see if that's a vocation you would like to pursue. Maybe this summer, we can go to a historical dig and see how they actually do it."

The dream remains alive, but guidance is offered without crushing the adventure involved. We can be realistic without being demeaning and insensitive.

The Dream Hoarders

There are many reasons people are uncomfortable sharing their dreams. Another one involves basic selfishness. We are too big or important to share. *I don't need your thoughts on matters of importance, but you need mine.*

How sad.

That attitude is in direct contradiction to the teachings of Jesus. You'd be surprised at how easy it is to find your life out of control when you become secretive.

Do you know someone like this? Are you wondering

why this person won't share his or her dreams? There are warning signs for this, too — the ones above we've discussed, and others:

- They develop a secretive nature.
- They make decisions without your input.
- Others know, but you don't.

One of the 15 specific sins mentioned in Galatians 5:20 is directly-related to individuals who won't share their dreams; it is *selfish ambition.* This Scripture says that those who live in that manner will not inherit the kingdom of God.

I'm not suggesting that you will be lost because you didn't tell your wife about the one wooded acre by the lake you bought. But that kind of attitude will lead to a pattern, and the pattern of withholding information will eventually sink you.

Maybe your dreams are not worthy of disclosure because they are full of selfish ambition. Maybe your parents aren't aware of them because they'd disapprove of your decision to quit college and join a rock band.

Not sharing dreams because they would find disfavor with our loved ones can open up a very messy can of worms.

A middle-aged husband that I knew about had always been interested in cars. Over the years, with the raising of three kids, he had to buy small, compact cars for driving to work. Recently, they had also purchased a mini van for transporting the kids to and from sports events and for vacations. His wife drove the van to her job, while he continued to drive a high-mileage compact.

Suddenly, he began to dream about owning a sports car, *If I don't get a sports car now, I'll never own one,* he thought. *College tuition will eat up any extra money, and then we'll be saving for retirement.*

Cautiously he approached his wife about his dream, but she quickly shot it down as totally selfish, impractical, and a waste of money in light of their son's entering college the next year.

As a salesman, he began to put aside money from his commissions in a secret account. Finally, when he had enough for the down payment, he called the local car dealer and ordered a green, two-seater sports car with leather interior.

One day while talking with his brother-in-law on the phone, he mentioned that he had ordered his new car. Later, the brother-in-law asked his wife if she was excited about getting the new car. Flabbergasted and embarrassed at not knowing, the wife blew up at her husband.

"I was going to tell you," he said. "I just wanted it to be a surprise."

For days she refused to talk to him and cried whenever one of the kids mentioned "the car."

Her sister wisely advised her, "Don't spoil this for Sam. The deed is done. Let him enjoy it. If you don't, you will only make things worse. Forgive him and put it behind you. It's not worth ruining your marriage over."

Finally, when the car arrived and he drove it into the driveway, the kids all ran out to inspect it and take turns going for a spin. The wife refused to even look at the car or ride in it. She acted as if it didn't exist.

This has continued for months, and the rift between them grows wider and wider. Short of a miracle or professional counseling, their marriage may not last to see their kids graduate from college. And if it does, they will surely go their separate ways once they no longer have a reason to stay together.

Both were in the wrong. He for being secretive; she for thinking that his dream was not worthy of consideration.

Why Dreams Die

I always have shared my dreams with Mildred. My dream that someday I would host a television program. My dream that God would give me the opportunity to be a part of healing hearts. What are your dreams?

A reluctance to share involves lack of faith in people. If you fail to share your visions of the future for your family, you are demonstrating that you lack faith in their input. You are really saying they aren't important enough to help decide what shape your dream will take.

There is hardly a more clear way to show contempt for your fellow man.

What many don't realize is that closing themselves off is almost a blatant invitation for temptation.

If you refuse to listen to your loved ones dreams of the future — for whatever reason — your loved one might find another person at their place of work who will be all too anxious to listen to his heart. The potential for that is pretty clear.

We must come to a place where we realize we are not the beginning and ending. Only One is Alpha and Omega. Our limited minds can conceive of some things — great, at times — but until we submit our will to God, this arrogance chokes us like vines.

And then the dreams die.

It is tough to get through life today without misunderstandings and strong differences of opinion, but that's where we must be like the prodigal son, who said, "I will arise and go." And he re-traced his steps to God and the earthly father he had forsaken.

The prodigal realized that when he turned his back on his home and set out to fulfill the dreams he had secreted in his heart that everything he truly loved was gone. He hadn't consulted his father and asked for wise counsel before embarking on this selfish journey. He merely said, "I'm going, and if the old man doesn't like it, I'll be so far away, he'll never find me."

When we think we're always right, we cut ourselves off from fellowship with God and expose ourselves to serious spiritual difficulties, oppression, and attacks from the devil.

This story of the prodigal son is a great example of the restoration that can occur when we have the courage to discard our bad attitudes. After the prodigal son was met by his father, they had a great feast with the members of the household.

From that point, the story passes into history, getting jumbled in with the masses of personal stories that have followed. But I like to think that son learned a valuable lesson and became much more open with his family. I am sure his dreams and goals from that point on didn't end up in the pigpen!

Keeping Dreams Alive

When a dream originates in your heart and mind, you have a dream that is truly a dream. Perhaps it hasn't unfolded before your eyes yet. That's when the sharing of dreams is hard.

You're afraid someone will think your dream is foolish or impractical. Keeping your vision to yourself might result in your life remaining in a holding-pattern, never growing.

Like minds, striving to embrace the spirit of God, are what bring righteous dreams to fruition. It keeps a relationship alive and vibrant. Believe it!

What can you do to keep your own dreams and those of the ones you love alive? Here are a few suggestions:

- Risk sharing your dreams.
- Ask the ones you love to tell you their dreams for the future.
- Be encouraging and supportive.

It is exciting to share in the dreams of what God can do in each of us. Everyone has an idea. Tell someone about it. It's so invigorating. Loving is also sharing your dreams with someone you love.

When you share your dreams with your loved ones, the dream may begin to take a different shape as they give their input and ideas. You will need to be open to suggestions and even allow your dream to change to include the one you love.

Once you have shared your dreams, your loved one may feel more comfortable opening up to you. To set the stage, you might say, "What would you like to do with your life if you could do anything you wanted?"

Your spouse may not open up immediately, but give it time. As your questions are mulled over in the days to come, they may realize that there is a dream hidden deep within the heart.

If the dream is much different from yours, pray for a spirit of unity to develop between you that will bridge the gap and allow you to converge your dreams into one.

From Dreams to Reality

A woman in our church had always dreamed of being a missionary to a foreign country. But as the mother of four children and with a husband tied to his job, Pam's dream appeared to be a long shot. Over the years, she taught Sunday school, served on the mission board of her church, and went on short-term mission trips. After a brief mission trip to Africa, her desire to become a missionary grew stronger than ever.

She shared her dream with her husband, but Ted had no desire to leave his job or to serve the Lord overseas. Instead of constantly harassing or condemning him, she began to pray that God would change his heart.

When Pam learned about a group traveling to Russia to minister, she mentioned it to her husband. He said, "No, although I'm interested in Russia, I don't think it's the right time."

Disheartened, Pam continued to pray.

A few months later Ted's mother died, and he had to

travel to the Caribbean to sell her island home. Because of a recent hurricane, the house had been severely damaged, and the family decided to relocate there for a year to oversee the repairs.

During that time, they met the director of a YWAM (Youth With a Mission) base on the island. Realizing that Ted was an accountant and a computer expert, the director asked, "Would you come and help us straighten out our accounting system?"

He agreed and became friends with the missionary group serving there.

One day, Ted mentioned that he had always wanted to go to Russia, but the time had never seemed right.

"Really?" the director asked. "We're preparing a team of local pastors for a trip to Russia next month. Would you like to go along?"

Finally, the reluctant husband was off on his first missionary journey.

After Ted's return, the mother's house was sold, and the family prepared to move back to the States.

"I don't think I'll go back to my old job," he told his wife as they packed. "Maybe we should look into joining YWAM and take their discipleship training course."

Today, the entire family is in training to become missionaries. Their destination is not yet known, but Pam's dream — which is now also her husband's — is finally becoming reality.

Conclusion

What are your dreams? "Your old men will dream dreams, your young men will see visions . . ." (Joel 2:28).

How about you? Why not attempt something great for God and for others? If we are only living for ourselves, we really do not have a lot to live for. You only pass this way once.

11

Financial Problems

A tithe of everything from the land, whether grain from the soil or fruit from the trees, belongs to the Lord; it is holy to the Lord.   Lev. 27:30

Problems with finances are the number one cause of divorce or marital strife in this country. I don't think anyone would argue with that assessment. There is hardly a household around that hasn't been touched by this problem.

I would like you to consider one concept, though, as we look at situations with loved ones who have problems in the area of finances.

Some wives call us and say, "My husband buys a $500 rifle and fishing tackle so he can go hunting and fishing. But if I want to get new drapes and a bedspread, which are for both of us, he tells me that I'm always spending too much money."

At Christmas time, a husband will expect a shirt, a tie, or a sweater, but he will buy his wife a set of bowls for the kitchen or a new washing machine. That principle does not fly. What if your wife bought you a new hammer and shovel? These are shared necessities.

Who Has Money Problems?

How can we tell if someone we love has a money problem? Here are a few behavior patterns that indicate they don't know how to handle finances.

- They are spending their money on the wrong things.
- They have not learned the principle of giving and receiving.
- They insist on "handling their own affairs."

Let me give you an example on a large scale of someone who has a money problem because it's being spent on the wrong things.

At PTL, the spending got out of control. Now, don't get me wrong—the ministry supported many charitable causes. More than anyone could imagine, Jim Bakker had a loving, giving heart. Jim Bakker expanded the ministry out of a genuine love for people.

At one time, Heritage USA was the third largest tourist attraction in the country. We were seeing huge crowds. But the "bigness" alone demanded more and more spending. This created cash flow problems in all areas, and forced the ministry to exist by crisis money management. It didn't have to be that way. The money was coming in to support the ministry, but spending was out of control. And I assume my responsibility for that, and I blame no one else.

If your loved one has a problem with spending money on the wrong things, don't automatically assume the motive is wrong. He or she might be trying to do the right things. They just have no direction. I know that has been true in my life.

Giving and Receiving

There are two types of people in the world: givers and takers.

If your loved one has a money need, it probably stems from a refusal to tithe, to give, to be generous.

The most fulfilled people in life are those who have learned to share with others. They have learned how to give and to do things for others. They are pouring out their lives for others.

The most miserable people are those who are self-centered and focused only on themselves. Most problems of not being able to fulfill our dreams stem from not having the finances to do it. We want to live in a better house. We want to pay for our grandchildren's college education, but we are not willing to give up something today to gain something better tomorrow.

"I'm so deep in debt, there's no way out."

When Elizabeth said that to me, it was the threat of her taking her own life that worried me the most. She had become so beaten and stretched out, that I knew she needed help. It was a constant struggle just to exist for her.

It was so difficult for her to understand she created her own problems. I shared with her the best way to have a worry-free marriage and right relationship is to only purchase what you can afford. If you don't have the money, don't buy it. The exception to this may be the home that you purchase, and if necessary, your automobiles. One of the ways to best assure a long, happy marriage is to pay cash for everything else.

My dear friend, Dr. E.M. Clark, told me about an incident that happened when he was raising money for a church in Illinois. The congregation had to move to a new location in order to expand, and needed $50,000 to get started. The future growth of their church depended on the success of this venture.

On Sunday morning Dr. Clark spoke to the congregation about giving and had just started to take commitments when a young man stood up and asked to speak.

He said, "My wife and I have been up most of the night praying, and God has definitely spoken to us about what we should do.

"We just sold our house," he continued, "and had $10,000 equity. We planned to buy another home and use the extra money as a down payment. God spoke to both of us and said, 'You can do better by giving the $10,000 to the church and renting for awhile.' "

His offer was shocking to Dr. Clark, to say the least, but God had obviously dealt with them.

Some months later Dr. Clark met the pastor of that church at a national meeting and asked him, "What happened to that young deacon and his wife who gave their down payment on a house to the building program?"

Smiling, he answered, "Brother Clark, you'd never believe what happened. About a month after they had given their money to the church, another local couple had to vacate their house in order to relocate for a much better job. They had no time to put their house on the market, so they offered it to our deacon and his wife if they would just take over the mortgage payments with no money down."

"That's wonderful," Dr. Clark replied, relieved to know God had blessed them.

"But there's more," the pastor continued. "The house was new, and the mortgage was less than our couple had planned to pay for an older home. They have moved in and are very happy."

It has been said that you can never out-give God. He always blesses us abundantly in return when we give out of obedience to His Word.

Setting the Record Straight

Since your loved one probably can't make the distinction between good and bad spending, just take them under your wing and make suggestions for handling finances.

If you do this from a "suggesting" posture, they will likely be more receptive. Don't barge in, waving your arms and demanding the checkbook. That humiliates and alienates.

Financial stability, or at least the application of the necessary principles, can be achieved in fairly short order. Your loved one will appreciate it, I guarantee that.

If the loved one hasn't yet applied the principle of giving and receiving, you have to realize that this problem involves a measure of selfishness. A person gets used to having his own way. Throughout childhood, he's never been told "no." As a result, an attitude develops that says, "If I want it, I should have it."

The longer we let them have their way, the more they will expect it. But there is a way out of this trap. Let's look at some ways you can help.

- Make them financially accountable.
- Help them set up a financial plan.
- Let them fail.
- Always be sure the Lord receives His tithe.

If you notice the problem of selfishness and arrogance in your loved one's financial affairs, point out to them the benefits of being *accountable* to someone. What do I mean by this?

If you are married, hopefully, you make financial decisions as a team. You are together on things. The husband is accountable to his wife, and the wife is accountable to her husband. If one knows what the other is doing with the money, it is very unlikely financial disaster will result. Sure, you'll have bumps along the money highway, but you won't wake up bankrupt one morning because your spouse squandered the family resources.

Accountability is a wonderful step toward a solution to financial problems.

The loved one with financial difficulties has probably never practiced accountability. Most of us need to be accountable to someone in financial matters. If the person in question is single, point out that there must be accountability to the bank where a car loan is negotiated.

My father is 99 years old. One of his best words of counsel to me as a child was never charge your current living expenses. If you don't have the money to buy something, save it and you'll always be ahead.

Mildred and I have never argued about money. Both of us are staunch believers in tithing and giving offerings above our tithing. And we've always followed my father's advice.

The only reason we use credit cards is for record-keeping purposes — not to charge for something we don't have the money for now. Each month we lay aside money in the bank for the car we will need in the future. So when the time comes to purchase it, we will have earned interest, instead of paying interest.

Sloppy handling of money establishes a pattern. It must be stopped early.

Teenagers and young adults who have not learned how to handle money will often tell their parents, "Just let me handle it myself."

Youthful pride wants to be left alone. But suppose your loved one has frittered away a summer's worth of earnings from his job. At that point, the parent must get involved and offer advice. If the pattern continues, their immediate future may be threatened. The young person must be made to understand that he, in fact, cannot handle a worsening money problem.

But how do you get him to the point where he will admit that he needs help?

Let him fail. Once.

You can talk all you want, but experience outweighs speeches. The person with a money problem must learn the lessons on his own. He must make a mistake or two.

Most people will see the problem at that point and climb out of the pit with just a little assistance. Your job is to stand over the pit and monitor the progress.

One way to do this is to help your loved one set up a financial plan and a budget.

First, ask them what their goals are for the future and how much it will cost to achieve those goals — whether its buying a car, going to college, getting married, or starting a business.

Once they have an objective in mind, you can help them budget their money, using the income they now receive. Without a financial plan to help them reach those goals, they will spend money as they please and end up being over-obligated in areas that will not benefit themselves in the long run.

There are plenty of good books on money management, some of which include pages for figuring out a budget. If you don't feel qualified to assist in this process, find someone you know who is financially responsible and who lives within their means. They will most likely be able to guide you and your loved one through the steps to financial freedom.

If, however, the problems are severe and involve extensive debt, you may want to consider going to a professional financial advisor for advice.

Conclusion

I am a fanatic on the subject of tithing. The only request I made of Mildred in handling our personal finances is that on the first of the month she writes the first check to pay our tithes. It has been my experience that people who do not . . . will not, and cannot pay their bills, and pay them on time. They don't tithe.

The same principle that helps us submit and come under control to pay our tithes is the same controlling spirit that will help us keep our spending habits in check. It is essential that we understand that God's blessing comes when we are seeking first His kingdom; then all the other things will be added.

I have always been certain also that our credit is excellent. Sadly, many Christians are poor credit risks because they have never brought themselves and their spending under submission.

God only knows how many divorces — how many damaged relationships in general — could be avoided by financial disclosure, whether it be on a personal level or corporate. We have discussed several character flaws involving secretive natures, but financial problems can be among the most embarrassing. It is of prime importance to rely on others for advice in this area, and to never be aloof in this matter.

12

Soul Preparation

For if the message spoken by angels was binding, and every violation and disobedience received its just punishment, how shall we escape if we ignore such a great salvation? Heb. 2:2-3

A few months ago, Mildred and I had the opportunity to return to my boyhood home. I was thrilled at the chance to see again the places where I played and laughed as a child. It was a time of great reflection in my life.

As I let these memories — distant and recent — swirl around in my head, I visited the church I attended as a child. Noticing the door to the basement of the church, I opened it and peered into the darkness, trying to decide if I wanted to negotiate the steep steps. A little of that adventurous boy of times past spurred me on, and I descended into this important room.

If you've ever stood in the basement of a church, you must know it can either be a frightful place or very quiet and peaceful. To me, it was a little of both because of the things I remembered.

Looking around under the light produced by a single bulb, I was reminded of so many things. A basement had been my refuge when scolded. It had also been the birthplace of many dreams. Emotions flooded my soul as I realized this is where many things began for me.

I thought about where my life had taken me. Satisfying mountain-top experiences and dark, dark valleys. The valleys I recalled vividly. My failures, my prison experiences, a cancerous kidney removed while an inmate.

I got to thinking about why people get off-track and lose their identity. Suddenly, I felt a powerful urge to pray. Weeping, I got on my knees and then lay down on the cold floor. I asked God to return me in my mind to a time when I first began to be aware of the meaning of life and His awesome power.

It had been the summer of my eleventh year. I remember sermons preached by our family's faithful pastor. He spelled out for us the reason for our existence on the planet. He paced about with his Bible open, and oh, how he taught. Finally, he looked out at the congregation and appeared to stare all of us in the eye! I will never forget what he said next.

"I tell you that our only goal in life should be to know God and share the gospel with the lost. We should cry out in our souls for the unreached among us. We should love them that much. And why? *Because Jesus is coming back!*"

Yes! Yes. I remembered the moment I surrendered my life to God. It was a moment of divine revelation for me.

It is by far the most important issue in this book, not for what Richard Dortch has to say, but for what our Lord taught us. "Everyone who has this hope in him purifies himself, just as he is pure" (1 John 3:3).

Do you care enough to help the one you love who does not have this blessed hope?

Where Are Your Priorities?

If only we could take this thought to heart: *Jesus will return.* It should be the most compelling, thrilling thought in our minds. How exciting it is to think of the Saviour's return!

It is also sobering because many will find themselves on the outside looking in. They will be like our ancestors in the Euphrates Valley who stood screaming in water up to their ankles, then their knees, waists, chests, heads — and Noah wouldn't hear them.

God won't hear those who have not accepted His way of escape. It will be too late. There isn't much time! It is a sobering thought.

Americans especially put such thoughts away and instead focus on parties, personal goals, work — anything but salvation. We have become masters at shutting down our hearts. And if we do think about it, who do we tell of Christ's love? For whom do we pray? Whom do we compel to come to Christ?

Strangers? Acquaintances?

What about those we love the most?

Many factors enter into our not taking the time with family members. We're waiting on someone else to talk to Uncle Herb about his soul preparation.

Maybe at some point, Uncle Herb hurt our feelings, and, yes, we've forgiven him but not to the point we actually want to tell him about Jesus. This is a situation I've encountered many times. Family members refuse to help a loved one, and a whole slate of justifications comes with it.

When we all stand before God, our petty differences here on earth aren't going to matter. All that will matter is whether we helped those we love prepare their souls for eternity. And by the way, "those we love" should include *everybody*.

Who Needs the Lord?

In most cases, it isn't difficult to recognize a person who *really* needs the Lord. He or she will either exhibit Christ-like behavior in their daily walk, or they will live like the devil.

This is the most clear concept in the universe — to be saved or lost.

Jesus wants us all to love Him. Forever.

Satan wants us all to perish. He wants to take us to hell with him — forever.

How can you recognize those who need the Lord?

- They are bound by sin.
- They have no peace in their lives.
- They are angry and bitter.
- They are not complimentary of the church.

Now, is it a hard decision? Do you want to bring the one you love to Christ? Do you care enough?

I understand if you are thinking about that one who gets his only enjoyment in life by tormenting the rest of the family. Perhaps it is a bitter aunt, determined to make as many miserable as possible. We all know people like this. But isn't that even more of an indication of their need for salvation?

It is very distasteful to approach a bully and offer a conciliatory handshake. It is against our nature. The question is, are your misgivings about approaching the lost going to matter in eternity? When we are in heaven, who is going to be there with us?

Our goal should be to bring as many as possible with us to heaven. The time is short! The sand is escaping the hourglass of history.

If you are afraid to approach an individual, try taking along someone who loves people and is skilled in helping others. If you're physically afraid, take *a strong person* of like faith with you. But do it. God won't wait much longer.

When You're Not Sure

The faith of some is not easily determined.

What about the dear, church-going aunt who volunteers at the soup kitchen, visits the sick in the hospital, and baby-sits her grandchildren so their mother can work?

How do you know whether she has accepted Christ as Saviour? She has never mentioned the name of Jesus or spoken of a salvation experience, and you aren't sure of the condition of her heart.

If you ask her, you are afraid she will be offended.

I know someone who faced this problem, but an opportunity was provided that opened the door for his loved ones to be saved.

Their church was presenting the drama, "Heaven's Gates and Hell's Flames." This fabulous light and sound show is presented throughout the United States and around the world many times each year in various churches, and thousands are saved.

People from the church hosting the drama are used as characters in the play, which depicts various situations involving people who die on the same day. The next scene shows those whose names are written in the Lamb's Book of Life entering into heaven and those who are lost being dragged by Satan and his demons into hell. The effect is quite dramatic with smoke and flames and screaming.

This man had a burden for his aunts and cousins, all of whom attended churches, but who had never indicated that they were born again. Since he did not see his relatives that often, he sent each of them an invitation to the play and included special tickets provided by their church. Then he and his wife began to pray.

On the first night of the drama, the church was packed and the pews were quickly being filled. The man kept praying, hoping his loved ones would arrive. Then, just as the drama was to begin, in walked his aunts and cousins. Making room for them on the pew, the man and his wife praised the Lord and waited for the results.

At the end of the dramatic presentation, the drama leader asked those who wanted to accept Jesus as their Saviour to raise their hand. Slowly, each one of his aunts and cousins raised their hands and indicated their desire to accept Jesus.

For days afterward, this man rejoiced in the Lord's faithfulness to answer his prayers for his lost loved ones. Although he did not know their spiritual condition, he took a step of faith and allowed God to use him to reach those he loved.

Conclusion

You can trust the Lord to show you the best way to tell your loved ones about Christ. Just be open and available and be willing to take that first step of faith. The Holy Spirit will do the rest, and you will have the assurance of knowing you and your loved ones will spend eternity together in heaven.

I recently heard a pastor say that in a hundred years, nothing will matter except where you are. Think of it. Someday soon, the greatest Man who ever lived will enter this world and return for the Church. He'll come back for me, and hopefully, He'll come back for you.

Will the disagreement you had with your neighbors matter much then? Will decades of hurt feelings make any difference?

I don't think they will.

There is work to be done in the coming days, and you are at the center of it, helping spread a message of love and hope to a lost world.

And to the one you love.

Dear Pastor Dortch,

 I want to know more about Life Challenge.

 I would like someone to contact me for spiritual counseling.

NAME _____

STREET _____

CITY, STATE, ZIP _____

PHONE _____

LIFE CHALLENGE
Office Hours 9 a.m. — 4 p.m., EST
Phone (813) 799-5433

(Fold here — staple and mail)

- -

┌ ─ ─ ┐
│   │
│ *stamp* │
└ ─ ─ ┘

Life Challenge
P.O. Box 15009
Clearwater, FL 34629